PERSUADE, DON'T PREACH

PERSUADE, DON'T PREACH

Restoring Civility across the Political Divide

KAREN J. TIBBALS, MBA, MA

Karen J. Tibbals, MBA (marketing), MA (religion)

Ethical Frames, LLC

Copyright © 2020 Karen J. Tibbals

ISBN: 978-1-7335749-2-1 (paperback)
ISBN: 978-1-7335749-3-8 (ebook)
ISBN: 978-1-7335749-4-5 (audiobook)
ISBN: 978-1-7335749-5-2 (workbook)
ISBN: 978-1-7335749-6-9 (leader's guide)

Published by
Ethical Frames, LLC
Website: www.PersuadeDontPreach.com
Email: Info@EthicalFrames.com

TABLE OF
CONTENTS

PREFACE

I WRITE THIS having just gotten back from seeing *To Kill a Mocking-bird* on Broadway. For those who don't remember, it is set in the 1930s in the South and illustrates the same tensions over race that we are experiencing today in the United States. It was written just about halfway in time between the American Civil War and today, and you can see progress has been made since then, but not enough. Some say that the divisiveness we are experiencing today is similar to the divisiveness we experienced before the Civil War, which is depressing.

Yes, we have made progress. But black men are still imprisoned at rates higher than whites for the same infractions, and black men are being shot on the streets for no reason. The frustration experienced with the lack of progress is as real today as it was in the 1930s.

I want to honor the progress and sacrifices people have made in the cause for social justice—sacrifices of time, money, and even their lives. I also want to honor those who have lost their lives and continue to lose their lives to violence, from the enslaved people before the Civil War, to the soldiers who fought for the freedom of the slaves, to the Civil Rights activists of the 1960s to today's social justice warriors.

In the play, Atticus Finch's approach of being respectful is called weak and meek by his son; ultimately, his lawful method is ineffective at achieving justice for Tom Robinson. I left the theater fired up to act. But then I wondered, what does this say about the approach I recommend in this book?

Because progress appears to be stalled today, or even have gone backward, I believe we need a new approach.

Like Atticus Finch, this book recommends respect—respect for people and for their values. But it recommends action also, in a new way, by using people's values to refocus on the issues. My approach is a new tool in the toolkit for social change, like nonviolence, and I hope it will be useful in helping us bring about change—change on the important issues of the day in a peaceful manner.

As Norman Vincent Peale once said: "Change your thoughts and you change your world." Let's get started changing things.

INTRODUCTION

T HE TITLE OF this book, *Persuade, Don't Preach*, represents the story arc of my life. I started my career in persuasion, working at an advertising agency and in marketing at major corporations. I ended that career when I left to go to seminary where I took a preaching course. This book represents the culmination of my learnings in all those places.

I left my job in corporate America at the end of 2011 to attend seminary and quickly ran smack into the culture wars. It's not that I had been oblivious; I had been working on teams that reported on trends for a long time. My experience in market research, insights, and strategy meant that I had read about the culture wars, but it was quite different to *live* in the middle of this left-right polarization.

I left suburban New Jersey (an area with expensive housing and a high cost of living) to move to a small city in the Midwest, which had almost the lowest-cost housing in the country. I left a job where I worked next to highly educated people of various ethnicities from all over the world, to shopping in stores and living next to laid-off factory workers or farmers—often people who didn't have the education or politics of my former colleagues. The stores were different, the restaurants were different, and the people spoke differently. It wasn't the language; it was the culture. I had gone from a Liberal culture where I felt comfortable, to a Conservative culture, which was very uncomfortable for me.

The school I was enrolled in and the church I attended were at ground zero of the political divide. Founded as a religious school, the school had become politically Liberal, and, as a result, it had lost support from some of the founding organizations that were Conservative. The church was in the process of being kicked out of a larger church organization because they had started welcoming LGBTQ members.

I had gone there to study how people made decisions about applying their beliefs to the rest of their lives, and I got a chance to observe it close up in real time! I went from trying to understand people's motivations as a work project, to trying to understand people's motivations in real time in order to understand what was going on around me.

In seminary, I found a theory that explained what was going on. It changed the way I looked at the world and at conflict. Up until then, I had always hated politics. But now that I have this insight, I look at politics in a fresh way. This book is intended to explain this insight to you and help you understand the new way I look at the world.

The insight I am describing here is invisible to us until we look at it differently. Just like fish not being aware that they are in water, or people not being aware that they are breathing oxygen, we aren't aware of our Ethical Zones™. They matter a lot—so much so that some people are willing to die for them.

Despite our strong commitment to these ideas, we don't think about them, we just react. It's only when we run into people who have different beliefs that we start to see that differences exist. But rather than appreciate what others bring, we judge others for having different beliefs. We call them prejudiced, immoral, and unethical, without trying to understand. When we don't understand the context that these beliefs arise from and what the beneficial parts of their belief system are, then we aren't being fair. Reading this book will open your eyes and bring you to a new level of understanding and give you a new way of talking to others—one that can help us restore civility.

WHY PREACHING DOESN'T WORK

IF YOU ARE like many people I have spoken to about this book title, you may be bristling at the word *preach*. Some people are moved by talented preachers, others take the title as an accusation, as an affront, thinking "not me, I don't preach!"

What I mean by preaching is when we talk only from our own perspective and don't take into account the other person's beliefs. We don't know how to talk to people across the political divide. Studies demonstrate that less than 10 percent of us can change our perspectives to consider the other person's belief structure, even when we are trying. That's true of both Conservatives and Liberals.

Instead of taking into account what the other person believes, we talk as though we are rehearsing our own beliefs. And that doesn't work. That's what I call preaching. And preaching only works for those who are already in the choir. This is why we talk past each other and why we (as a society) are frozen. That's behind the loss of civility.

The goal of this book and of the workshops and speeches that I give is to help people understand that there is another way to talk to each other and to equip them with the tools they need to start talking in another way.

OUR POLARIZED SOCIETY MAKES LISTENING TO EACH OTHER HARD. It's common knowledge that the first step in persuading someone is to listen. Dale Carnegie's recommendation from the 1940s to listen to the other person first is known broadly. But because of our polarized society today, even this step is hard.

I can't tell you the number of people whom I have heard say they try to listen to the other side, but they get outraged and stop listening. We need a new way to listen. This book will help you see what people say in a new way through the Ethical Frames you put on, which gives you a new way to listen.

SHAMING, BLAMING, AND NAMING DON'T WORK EITHER. I have heard people I respect say that they can wake people up and get them to pay attention to how bad their conduct is by naming their behavior. That's a variation on shaming. Shaming doesn't work. Research shows that shaming paralyzes people; it keeps them from acting in positive ways. As William Goldberg has said: "I have never seen a person grow or change in a constructive direction when motivated by guilt, shame and/or hate."

My point is that we don't want people to feel badly. We want people to act. So, name-calling and shaming don't help.

As D. W., a prison inmate said: "It seems obvious to me that rhetoric and blaming don't solve anything."

Consider this fable to help you understand what happens when we preach or shame.

One day the sun and the wind got into an argument about which was more powerful. They agreed to settle the argument by recognizing that the more powerful would be the one who made the traveler take off his cloak. The wind went first, sending a strong gust. That make the traveler hold onto his cloak tighter, wrapping it around himself and holding close.

Then it was the sun's turn. The sun shone brightly, warming up the traveler, until the traveler lay down to bask in the sun, taking off his cloak.

Preaching is like what happens when the wind blows strongly. The listener holds onto their beliefs even more tightly.

Academic research demonstrates that extreme actions by demonstrators have exactly the opposite effect than they want on people who disagree. The watchers tend to strengthen in their belief system, which is exactly what the protesters don't want. As Abigail Van Buren has said: "People who fight with fire, usually end up with ashes."

Let me emphasize this point: The very action that the demonstrators thought was so powerful has exactly the opposite effect than they want. The activists may be proud of themselves for being so formidable and forceful, and believe what they are doing is working, but they don't realize that what they are doing is actually counterproductive. Plus, the other side already knows basically what you think.

On the other hand, persuasion is what happens when the sun comes out. When we listen to someone who "gets us," who seems to come from our perspective, we relax. We listen differently. That person becomes part of our tribe. And if that person makes a surprising comment that fits with our belief system, we agree. That's what happens when the sun comes out.

> *The very action that the demonstrators thought was so powerful has exactly the opposite effect than they want.*

That's what this book is about. Learning how to take into account the other's perspective so that you can be convincing. It isn't easy to do, but the attempt is worth it.

HOW TO READ THIS BOOK

THIS BOOK DRAWS on several academic theories. It leans heavily on Jonathan Haidt's moral foundations theory but also uses Alan Fiske's relational models theory, Steven Pinker's views on rationality, and spiral dynamics developed by Clare Graves. But I don't just tell you these theories. I apply them to the issues that we are in conflict about today.

As you read this book, try to withhold the judgment you would normally make. You might be tempted to take this as an opportunity to get angry about those with whom you disagree and try to come up with arguments to convince people that your way is right.

Instead, try to approach this discussion as if you were an anthropologist studying the culture. Look for the truths behind the ideas that don't agree with your preexisting ideas. When we allow for the truth behind two conflicting ideas to emerge, it can lead us to a deeper truth. This is synthesis. Others call it paradox. In seminary, we called this thinking both/and. The idea is that there can be truth in two different ideas, and if that is true, then resolving the conflict can lead to important insights. Look for the glimpses of truth.

Also, think about the issues separately from the values and from the people. You need to decouple people themselves from what they believe and from the issues that arise out of their values. This book should help you separate them.

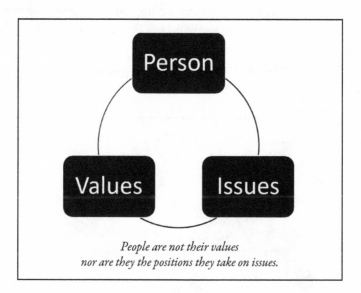

People are not their values
nor are they the positions they take on issues.

Use this also as an opportunity to understand yourself better as well as those you are reading about. Self-awareness will be helpful as you walk this path.

This is difficult work. It involves challenging some of your strongly held beliefs. It requires that you go beyond your normal motivated reasoning (everyone has this!). We need to approach this effort with humility. The world is a complicated place, and there are unexpected consequences to our actions. We may think we know the right action to take, but what if we are wrong? What if what we think is right actually makes matters worse?

Unintended consequences are real. Maybe you've heard about the cobra effect, which refers to a time when the British government in India offered a bounty for cobra corpses (because the country had too many cobras), leading to people breeding cobras. When the cobras were set free after the bounty ended, the country experienced an increase in cobras. Are there cobras in what you think should happen?

Hold onto your beliefs lightly.

THE STRUCTURE OF THE BOOK

THIS BOOK IS divided into three parts. Part I reviews the theories that the book is based on. This section will help you understand what is going on underneath the words you hear and the framework of the belief system that you can't see. After reading this section, you should understand both your own and others' Ethical Frameworks more clearly. You should also be able to start to tease apart the issues, the values, and the people.

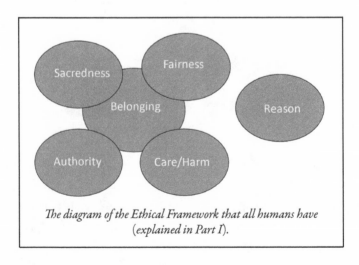

The diagram of the Ethical Framework that all humans have
(explained in Part I).

Part II looks at how the theories apply to the issues of our day so that you will be able to use the theories to better understand how people's opinions can be explained. Part III is the practical section, how you can apply this way of thinking in your personal life and persuade the people in your life.

PART I

THIS SECTION WILL review the various social science theories and research that explain the conflict in our society and why we are so divided. We all have the same Ethical Zones in common, which are invisible to us; we take them for granted. Conflict happens when two people place different importance on the Ethical Zones and/or have different interpretations of them.

Here you will start to be able to untangle the people from the issues and from the values.

By reading this section, you are putting on a new pair of glasses: Ethical Frames. You will never see the world in the same way again.

Conflict happens when two people place different importance on the Ethical Zones and/or have different interpretations of them.

WHO'S IN OUR CHOIR?
BELONGING AND
COMMUNITY

1

H OW WE FEEL about the group we belong to is one of the most powerful forces in the world. Jonathan Haidt recognized the power of belonging as one of the five areas in his book *The Righteous Mind: Why Good People Are Divided by Politics and Religion*. He uses the term *moral foundations* to describe the five areas, but I call them Ethical Zones because I have expanded his set to six. Later, I will add a seventh.

> *The group we belong to is not (usually) one we consciously choose. It is an outgrowth of our upbringing, our context, and our biology.*

Those of you who know the hierarchy of needs might recognize belonging as a key need described by Abraham Maslow.

Here's a graphic description of the Ethical Framework I describe in this book, with the first Ethical Zone, belonging, highlighted.

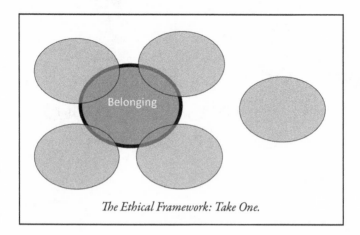

The Ethical Framework: Take One.

Belonging is at the center of the Ethical Zone Framework because the group you belong to drives *everything*; all the other factors I will describe depend on which community you belong to. We believe that we are acting as individuals and not as part of a community. But that is not true. We are unaware of how much identification with a group drives our attitudes.

I am using the words *belonging* and *community* instead of the word *loyalty* that Haidt uses because it doesn't have the same connotations. Part of my positive feelings about this Ethical Zone arises out of the importance my religious denomination places on community support. Besides that, I also confuse Haidt's use of the word here with loyalty to an authority figure, which is a separate concept. I think belonging and community is a clearer description of the totality of this Ethical Zone.

Community is an incredibly powerful force. It is so powerful that people with strong social connections have been shown to live longer, happier lives. That's important.

BELONGING: AN INCREDIBLY POWERFUL FORCE

THE BELONGING AND community factor has an evolutionary origin. Groups that had higher group participation were more likely to survive; thus, we humans are all descended from people who knew how to cooperate.

In the early stages of humanity's development, society consisted of small nomadic clans that shared food and other resources. They were the first expressions of belonging and community. The Ethical Zone of belonging and community has persisted throughout the centuries as a remnant of the survivors: us.

As part of this belonging, we pick up the beliefs of those we associate with, as a way to be part of the crowd. Sometimes, we are like chameleons.

Young children, for example, develop a strong sense of belonging very early in life, before they are verbal. Evidence for this includes the fact that young children spend more time looking at people who look similar to them, and that their mirror neurons light up when someone who is like them is pricked by a needle but not when the person is considered an other. In describing this effect, political scientist Lilliana Mason of the University of Maryland writes that all humans have a deeply rooted in-group bias.

The unconscious reaction that children exhibit continues into adulthood. Literally, our brains work differently for in-group members versus out-group members. Adults' saliva secretions vary also when an in-group member is sad compared to an out-group member, and their neurons react differently based on the social category of the face they see. These reactions happen fast—within 300 milliseconds!

A review of the xenophobia over the centuries in the US showed a range of targets, from Germans, to the Irish, to the Chinese, to the Mexicans, and, most recently, to Muslims. These in-groups may be based on race, but not always. There have been numerous wars fought and massacres where there were no racial differences, such as World War I in Europe where the German Kaiser was related to the English royalty, and the African conflict in Rwanda and Burundi between the Hutu and the Tutsi whose differences were economic, not ethnic.

Psychologist Kristin Pauker has been studying prejudice in a society in which there is no dominant race—Hawaii. As an opinion piece about her work in the *New York Times* recounted, perceptions of in-group bias in Hawaii are not racially based the way they are on the mainland. However, even in multiracial Hawaii, the article makes it clear that nonracial forms of in-group "othering" have arisen. It's hard to get away from othering, even if it isn't based on race.

The group we belong to is not (usually) one we consciously choose. It is an outgrowth of our upbringing, our context, and our biology. People brought up in societies where there is scarcity grow up to be more Conservative, to value what they have, and try to figure out ways to keep it. People who grow up in prosperous environments look to fix what they think is wrong, assuming that they can keep the best parts of what they grew up with. This last group tends to be Liberal.

Those with stronger ties to an in-group (more likely Conservatives) use similar portions of the brain for both the group and themselves; those with less strong ties don't. Conservatives have brain responses when they see people in their in-group being sad that are similar to their own sadness, but not when the person is from the out-group. People who sweat more when they see pictures of those in an out-group are more likely to discriminate against them.

Some of the most overt displays of belonging that we see today are in allegiance to sports teams and in the intense bonds that are formed among army buddies. Negative events such as battles and being under attack, like during 9/11, may create stronger bonds within a group.

Thinking about sports and war brings in another important aspect of belongingness: winning. What is important to those in a group is that the group wins. Winning boosts the sense of cohesion.

THE DOWNSIDE OF BELONGING

THE EFFECTS OF belonging and community are not all positive; one of the downsides of belonging is conformity. The belonging effect is so dominant that people will make errors if the group around them makes errors; accuracy doesn't matter.

For example, people misidentify colors or line length when the people around them give erroneous information and switch their position on an issue if they are told that their group feels a different way. It doesn't even have to be a group that you have strong ties to. Even an insignificant group membership can have this effect. This is probably a contributing factor to people believing so-called fake news.

Sometimes it seems that my entire life has been one in which I feel outside of the group I am part of, and it is uncomfortable. When I went to seminary and became part of the community there, I brought with me the beliefs I had when I was part of the corporate world. I was a mature student, so I had held those beliefs for decades. Because I didn't discard those beliefs, I didn't fit in at seminary. I was regarded with suspicion, especially by the younger students (who were the same age or younger than my son).

I've heard of others who made a similar transition as I did, but, unlike me, they conformed, abandoning their previous beliefs and fit in at seminary better than I did.

On the other hand, people leave groups all the time when their beliefs don't match the group. I could have transferred to a different seminary where I fit in better, but I didn't. Instead, I stuck it out and was gradually accepted for who I was. This decision led to personal growth and an emerging sense of what I wanted to do with my seminary degree.

My lesson from this experience is that choosing a group is somewhat where you find yourself and somewhat an individual decision—that we choose which group fits us best. But still another part is how individuals deal with the feelings of not belonging. Leaving is one option, as is changing your beliefs to conform.

Another downside of the belonging and community Ethical Zone is that those who do not belong to a particular group are considered an out-group. This results in othering—in other words, regarding those who aren't part of our group as less worthy, or less deserving, or even less human. Winning over the out-group becomes important. And winning leads to a burst of dopamine, the hormone that gives us pleasure.

Too often, we choose a group because they hate the same people we do—or common enemy belonging. A false sense of belonging is provided when you have a common enemy. Research has been shown that those with strong allegiance to a sports team enjoy when the opposite team experiences bad luck. Germans have a word for this: *schadenfreude*.

That is not real community. It is fake, and it fades easily. It's the fast-food version of belonging, the same as gossip. It feels addictive in the moment, but it doesn't elevate you. Such belonging is tainted and impure. It does not provide the same benefits of community as real belonging.

Twentieth-century black poet Langston Hughes articulated the effects of hatred on a person when he asserted, "Ever'thing there is but lovin' leaves a rust on yo' soul."

In a later chapter, I will discuss community in a new way that transcends the downsides of belonging.

THE RISE OF INDIVIDUALISM

THE BELONGING BONDS in society have been loosening recently. Research shows that Americans are the most independent of any country's people and are becoming more isolated and independent. In his book *Bowling Alone: The Collapse and Revival of American Community*, Robert Putnam documents a decline in civic participation in institutions, churches, and neighborhood communities.

Americans have lost trust in their institutions. This has resulted in a loss of what is called social capital.

In the US, our levels of loneliness are double what they were in the 1980s. This is considered to be an epidemic of loneliness, not just in the US but in the developed world. Lack of community is considered to be a contributing factor to what are now called deaths of despair—addiction and suicide.

Ann Case and her collaborator, Nobel Prize–winner Angus Deaton, have documented the rise of those deaths among white men in America. The negative health effects of feeling isolated have been estimated to be equivalent to smoking fifteen cigarettes a day.

Belonging is so crucial that it affects an individual's self-esteem. Research shows that those who strongly identify with a group find their identity in that group, and when the group loses, their self-esteem plummets.

There are variations in the degree to which these social belonging bonds have loosened. Those who moved less (such as those who stayed in rural areas) have higher levels of belonging than those who moved away. This is self-perpetuating, as those who have moved less are less likely to move in the future. Their strong community ties give them a social safety net that can't be duplicated in cities.

Those who stayed in the place they were born tend to be higher in belonging to a physical community and tend to be Conservative in their outlook. They have stronger participation in group activities. The reluctance of Conservatives to move appears to have contributed to a recent decline of the moving rate to the lowest level in recent history.

On the other side of the political aisle, Liberals are more likely to have moved away, loosening their ties. That doesn't mean Liberals don't have a sense of a group that they belong to; it's just different and not (as much) the place they are from. When I make this point in my presentations, I show a group of three people sitting together on a park bench all looking at their phones. The people are together physically, but their focus is on being with people who aren't there physically.

A clear expression of this difference between loosening of place-based identification is found in patriotism attitudes. Liberals tend to consider themselves citizens of the world, while Conservatives are more likely to consider themselves citizens of the place they live in and the country they live in.

For example, few white-collar workers in cities (a bastion of liberalism) know people who are in the armed forces; the armed forces are filled with people from Conservative rural areas and those from the disadvantaged minority classes, who also tend to be more Conservative. Veterans who attend college feel unwelcome and criticized by the Liberal college students they attend classes with.

Liberal young tech workers at Google protested when their company won a national defense contract; they don't want to work on it. In Britain, leaving the European Union was favored by those with a high sense of place and opposed by those in the cities.

Effects of Changes on Our Community

Changes in how we work and shop have affected the degree of involvement we have with our community. The loss of retail is one these changes. The rise of internet shopping, accelerated by Amazon, has led to the demise of retail stores in the US, where we would run into others from our local communities. Now we get many items delivered and have less occasion to interact with others in the physical world.

The internet has also led to an increase in remote working or telecommuting, another lost opportunity to intermingle with others in the real world. People interview for jobs via video chat, which doesn't provide as many cues about people skills as in-person interviews. Many efforts are made to try to provide substitutes for this loss, but they are always second best.

Changes in eating and shopping habits have also led to the demise of the local bakery in small villages in France. These bakeries often served as a community center, a place for villagers to gather in the early morning and catch up on the news, but the rise of the hypermarket and the trend to eating less bread has made the village bakery business unworkable in some villages.

Further, there has been an increase in social sorting—people are more likely to live with others just like them and marry people just like them. Social sorting has become so strong that people don't want their children to marry someone whose political beliefs are different. So instead of sharing a community with people of different backgrounds and different beliefs, getting to know them, and giving them the benefit of the doubt, we have fewer broad community ties with a variety of people.

As we stopped encountering a variety of other people, we lost our motivation to be civil to those we disagree with.

SOCIAL MEDIA CAUSE LOWER FEELINGS OF BELONGING

SOCIAL MEDIA IS one factor driving us apart and causing some of us to substitute online interaction for in-person interaction.

Humans desire connection so deeply that we use any way we can to try to satisfy that need, even if that way isn't effective at satisfying that need. In fact, research demonstrates that social media have the opposite effect of in-person contacts, with a negative effect on psychological well-being, including an increase in depression. The happiest people are those who have the strongest in-person social relationships, not those with the most likes or the most followers.

Our social media choices that substitute for in-person interaction are also contributing to an increase of alignment of worldview with political views. There used to be conservative Democrats and liberal Republicans, but that distinction is disappearing.

There is now a beginning of an awareness that social media can't substitute for what some call the meat world or IRL (in real life). This was demonstrated in a survey in Britain that measured the sense of community. Local communities were rated at 82 of 100 points, the local news media at 54, and social media at 34, a huge difference.

This rising awareness of the need for community plays out in different ways. A sign on the streets of Spokane, Washington, calls out that the local coffee shop was "local before local was cool." The rise of coworking spaces is attempting to take advantage of the need to belong. The perhaps too-ambitious goal of the We company (whose most well-known division is WeWork) was "to transform society by creating a sense of community," which was expressed in the use of the word *community* 150 times in the documents for their aborted IPO.

Facebook groups substitute for actual groups. Apps for phones often state they are working to develop community. The exercise firm Peloton attempts to provide a simulation of community to those who don't leave their home through video workouts. But as was just discussed, the online world can't really substitute for real-life interactions.

To counteract this epidemic of loneliness, doctors in Europe are starting to prescribe participating in social and community activities for depressed or anxious people. In a TED Talk in 2019, Johann Hari told the story of the effect of one such prescribed group in East London. It was so challenging to one anxious woman that she threw up before attending. But over time bonds have been built and the group has thrived, working together to learn how to create a garden. That woman no longer throws up before the meetings.

POLITICAL PARTIES ARE THE NEW CHOIR

POLITICS HAS BECOME the new religion.

Both religion and politics are sources of belonging and identity. People are passionate about both of them. People are willing to die for both of them. Both involve beliefs and values. Both can turn mean-spirited. Politics has merged with religion on the right and substituted for religion on the left.

Both sides preach—in different ways, but they both preach. By preaching I mean that they are so caught up in their own beliefs that they are not open to beliefs of others.

Today, a growing number of people identify as spiritual but not religious. Even those who do identify with a religion often don't attend services. The religious world watches as their congregations age and their churches empty out and close. Instead of identifying with a religion, people align with a political party.

Michael Gerson at the *Washington Post* summed it up this way: "The merging of politics and religion transforms opponents into enemies. It turns compromise into heresy."

Lilliana Mason of the University of Maryland suggests that the factors of social sorting, independence, and isolation, together with social media, are responsible for the increasing degree to which people rely on their political identity for their sense of belonging. Social sorting is so strong that interest in a potential date declines if the person is identified as from the other political party.

Differences between the Choirs

The differences between Liberals and Conservatives play out throughout their lives. Not only does it affect the issues they support and the media they consume, affiliation affects the food they eat and the words they use.

While there is a spectrum of belief, the core of Liberals' beliefs are that businesses make too much profit, that the economic system unfairly favors powerful interests, that America's openness to people from all over the world is essential to who we are as a nation, that abortion should be legal in most cases, that there are significant obstacles for women to get ahead, and that affirmative action is valuable.

They also believe that a core value of the US is its ability to change. The paradox is that Liberals are relatively anti-capitalism, but liberalism only has developed in capitalistic countries. Thus, growing up in a rich world capitalistic economy means taking the benefits of it for granted and wanting improvements on the status quo.

On the other side of the political aisle, core social Conservative beliefs focus on the reliance on long-standing principles: that government shouldn't provide many services, that the country should follow its own interests even when allies disagree, and that we risk losing our country's identity if we are too open to people from other countries.

At its core, the difference is that Conservatives want to conserve the past, while Liberals believe change is positive. Another key belief is that Conservatives look to individual action to solve problems, while Liberals believe that the structure of society has to change to solve problems. Conservatives believe that when government intervenes, individuals stop helping others. The irony is that both Conservatives' and Liberals' views have some validity.

A signal of belonging is the media you consume. Fox News is an obvious choice for Conservatives; MSNBC is the choice of Liberals. There are differences in which TV shows people watch and how they use social media. Liberals watch shows like *Black-ish*, *Broad City*, *The Good Place*, and *Will and Grace*. Conservatives (mostly) watch very different shows. They are more likely to watch shows such as *The Brave*, *Blue Bloods*, *Lethal Weapon*, and *NCIS*, as well as reality-based shows like *The Apprentice* and *Shark Tank*. *Dancing with the Stars* and *Star Trek* are some of the few shows that both groups watch.

The words that Liberals and Conservatives use about the feeling of belonging are different. Conservatives might use words with a positive connotation such as *loyalty*, *patriot*, and *homeland*, and negative words such as *deserter*, *deceiver*, *foreign*, and *betrayal*. Liberal words for this zone might include *communal*, *group*, and *solidarity*.

Both use words like *treason* and *treacherous*. To Liberals, the words *foreign* and *immigrant* are not negative, but to Conservatives they are. This means that when you work on how to talk to someone you disagree with, the words that signal belonging need to be chosen carefully.

In terms of the food we eat, Liberals prefer a sharper and more distinct taste profile than Conservatives. Liberals eat arugula and kale; Conservatives eat iceberg lettuce. The fact that President George H. W. Bush didn't like broccoli fits perfectly with the taste profile preferred by Conservatives. Conservatives drink light beer; Liberals, IPAs (India pale ales).

Liberals are more likely to be vegetarian. Conservatives are more likely to eat at both fast-food and other chain restaurants such as Arby's, Applebee's, Cracker Barrel, and Burger King. Liberals don't (at least as much). Patronizing national brands and chain restaurants conveys that you belong to the Conservative tribe. Not using national brands and instead following the latest trends are signals that you belong to the Liberal tribe. That's why there were so many chain restaurants where I went to school in the Midwest.

When a new ethnic restaurant opened, the Liberals at the college would rally around to try to support it. Unfortunately, there weren't enough Liberals to support these new ethnic restaurants, and the Conservatives wouldn't consider them, so many of the ethnic restaurants would eventually close.

Companies are Picking a Choir

In 2018, Nike tried to make the power of belonging work for them. They jumped into a preexisting conflict with both feet by using Colin Kaepernick as the face of the thirtieth anniversary Just Do It campaign. Two years earlier, Kaepernick started trying to draw attention to the killings of unarmed black men (which the Black Lives Matter movement tried to bring awareness to) by kneeling during the national anthem instead of standing at attention.

A year later, Kaepernick was out of a job and had sued the NFL for colluding in not hiring him. Other athletes began imitating him, leading the NFL to institute a policy requiring athletes to stand during the national anthem. This was a conflict between players who are mostly either Liberal or from an ethnic minority group and the owners who are more Conservative.

President Donald J. Trump weighed in on the issue, scolding players for disrespecting the flag. Conservatives see it as a patriotism issue, with half of Trump supporters saying they would boycott NFL games over the protest; on the other hand, Liberals are cheering for the attention being paid to an issue they feel needs that attention.

The NFL ban didn't stand very long; they reversed themselves after the controversy erupted. The NFL was caught between Conservatives, who are more likely to watch televised sports, and the Liberals, who don't. There were high emotions on both sides.

So, when Nike decided to jump into this emotionally charged issue, they had to know they were walking into a difficult situation. Their brand had been lagging among younger consumers (who are more likely to be Liberal) and among ethnic consumers. The emotional power of taking Colin Kaepernick's side helped Nike to signal that they were on the side of those Liberal and ethnic customers. It didn't matter much to Nike that white Conservatives set their shoes on fire and threatened to boycott the company; those people weren't going to buy Nikes anyway.

This has worked out for Nike as I write this in early 2020. Nike sales were up 7.5 percent after a previous decline.

Gun Control Has Become a Marker of a Subtribe

Unlike Nike, Dick's Sporting Goods tried to avoid the emotional power of a highly charged issue when they announced that they would no longer sell assault rifles and would restrict sales of guns to those over twenty-one after the Parkland shooting in February 2018. Dick's tried to soften the impact on Conservatives by including a line in their press release about supporting the Second Amendment. Further, in interviews, the CEO went on TV shows to say that he is a gun owner himself. They were relying on facts, on reason and rationality.

But when it was discovered that Dick's had contributed money to a gun-control lobbyist, there was a backlash. The NRA came out against Dick's, and some major gun manufacturers decided not to sell guns to Dick's.

Why did the NRA and its supporters have this extreme reaction? I have been struggling with this question as I have been working on this book, but I am Liberal, so it's not surprising that I don't understand. I finally found a clue in the book *Braving the Wilderness* by Brené Brown. Because she grew up in gun culture, she understands that culture in a way I can't.

Brown explained that it isn't necessarily the guns themselves; it is what the guns represent to that group. Guns have come to be part of what it means to be an American, so if you are Conservative, that represents the belonging and community Ethical Zone. Without quite realizing what was happening, because our own beliefs are invisible to us, Dick's was stepping into the belonging and community Ethical Zone and it exploded, despite their best efforts.

How has this affected Dick's? Sales were down, in a year they should have done well, because their major competitor, Sports Authority, went out of business. It has taken an entire year for Dick's retail sales to recover, but they have.

Delta Airlines also got caught in a gun-control blowback, which may also have had an impact on where Amazon put their second headquarters. After the Parkland shooting, Delta eliminated a discount they had been providing to NRA members. The pro-gun members of the Georgia state legislature punished Delta for this by eliminating a fuel-tax exemption that would have saved Delta millions of dollars. This move didn't just affect Delta; the other airlines who fly out of the Atlanta hub lost their exemption as well.

While this action by the Georgia state legislature could be perceived as being self-serving and rational (Georgia gets more money if they eliminate the exemption), the legislature was warned that the action could negatively affect perceptions of Georgia as a business-friendly state.

The Ethical Zone of belonging is such a strong force that legislators didn't heed that warning. Interestingly, their decision may also have had an impact on Amazon's choice of HQ2. Atlanta had been in the running for the Amazon HQ2, but Amazon didn't choose Atlanta, and instead initially decided to split their HQ2 into two cities: Long Island City in Queens, New York, and Crystal City, Virginia. (Note: They later abandoned the NY location.)

Did the state legislature's decision about Delta impact the Amazon decision? We may never know, but it could have.

Levi's is approaching gun control in the same way that Nike approached the NFL issue. Levi's wants to make themselves more attractive to younger consumers, so they are using the issue of gun control to communicate they are for young people. Interestingly, they say they are being inclusive and appear not to realize that those who had a problem with Dick's would have the same problem with them. Levi's efforts have pushed Republicans to prefer the other dominant brand, Wrangler.

Masculinity Is a Subtribe

Gillette waded into the masculinity arena with its February 2019 video #ToxicMasculinity. This one-and-a-half-minute video opens with audio about "toxic masculinity" and the #MeToo movement. The voiceover then raises the question of whether "boys will be boys" should still be the norm and asks, "Is this the best a man can get?"

The response on the internet has been strident, with indignant men vowing never to buy Gillette products again, among a chorus of sentiments such as, "Spare us your sermons." The over one million dislikes on YouTube probably came from Conservative men; the men who like the sentiment are probably Liberal.

Gillette has been in a difficult position, with sales eroding because of new brands like Dollar Shave Club and Harry's. Gillette had been losing the younger generation to these hipper new brands. This video didn't save the brand; Procter & Gamble wrote down the value of the Gillette brand by $8 billion a few months after the video aired. There was a chorus of rejoicing at the Gillette write-down in comments on YouTube. Gillette sales have started to rebound with the introduction of new products.

So, who is in the choir that is reacting so negatively to Gillette's video? Of course, these negative reactions are coming from men who are Conservative. The reaction by Conservatives highlights another key part of belonging: your gender.

Gender is one of the first ideas you learn as a child, about which sub-tribe you belong to: male or female. Thus, it's not surprising that challenging the definition of masculinity (read: challenging the belonging that Conservative men feel) created a storm among those who think the definition of masculinity is just fine the way it is. Men are more likely to be politically Conservative, so this isn't surprising. And recent research seems to indicate that men who feel insecure about their masculinity may be the most likely to defend it in a politically charged way—exactly the way that men responded to the Gillette video.

Of course, Liberals disagree, which is another reason why this is in the belonging and community Ethical Zone and sets up a trap on the other side. In fact, Liberals are championing the idea of rethinking masculinity, taking it even further, seeing it as a crucial part of making the world a safer place for gays and trans people.

An example of this Liberal movement is a panel discussion at Cannes in 2018 entitled "The Future of Masculinity" by Faith Popcorn's Brain Reserve. The website for the accompanying zine states that it is "exploring how masculinity is evolving." Brain Reserve's remit is to focus on future trends, which they read from Liberals. The masculine Conservative choir is ignored.

In the next chapter, I will discuss how another Ethical Zone (respect for authority) contributed another powerful emotion that helped make these masculinity efforts even more explosive.

As I will discuss in later chapters, belonging interacts with the other zones. Those who belong to the same choir are more likely to be viewed as sacred, more likely to deserve more, more likely to be cared about, and more likely to be respected as leaders and authority figures. Because President Obama is biracial, he didn't belong to the white in-group, and thus was less likely to be respected as a legitimate president by Conservatives, who have stronger in-group identification.

PREACHING TO THE CHOIR

THIS CHAPTER HAS just reviewed the two choirs that exist in the US and the rest of the rich world. When we preach to our own choir, we reflect those values and it works pretty well. What we don't know how to do is to convince the other choir of our point of view.

One researcher has said that our efforts at persuasion don't work because we are not asking the person to change their mind on an issue; rather, we are asking them to change their values. I would add, we are asking them to change their allegiance to their tribe, which actually means asking them to change their identity. That's a big ask, and rarely works.

There is another way that works at least some of the time, which this book will address in Part III.

Cultural Differences

A limitation of this book is that it is focused on the dominant culture in the US and the developed world. Most of what is included doesn't apply to the various religious and ethnic groups in the US, such as blacks, Latinos, Asians, and Muslims. Unlike whites in the US, these groups haven't undergone the shift to have their politics align with their underlying Ethical Zones.

Although these ethnic groups may *politically* align with Liberals, they themselves are not Liberal in many of their attitudes. The *Saturday Night Live* "Black *Jeopardy!*" sketch, which appeared right before the 2016 election, captured this dynamic by highlighting how similar experiences and attitudes are between the white working class and blacks, despite the prejudice whites feel against blacks as an out-group.

Because ethnic groups are out-groups, they become the target of common enemy belonging for Conservatives. On the other hand, the politics of ethnic groups are more clearly what is called identity politics. Identity politics occurs when your ethnicity itself drives your political views. Thus, the Nike Colin Kaepernick campaign has two different forces behind it: identity politics for minority ethnic groups and the power of the Ethical Zone of belonging for both white Liberals and white Conservatives.

The political alignment of ethnic groups and Liberals may be unstable, because their Ethical Frameworks are different. The concepts in this book should help Liberals not just understand Conservatives differently, it should also help Liberals understand the differences between their viewpoint and their politically aligned ethnic partners who are more Conservative at heart. On the other hand, if you are from a minority group aligned with Liberals, this book should help you understand the dominant culture more fully.

Note that in this book I flip back and forth between two different sets of terminology: Liberals and Conservatives and Republicans and Democrats. These groups have overlapping memberships, but they are not identical. I have chosen the terms carefully in order to be true to the data behind what I say.

A further caveat: Americans (and people from other developed countries) have different viewpoints than those of people from less developed countries. The researchers who documented this skew have called the developed world phenomenon WEIRD: Western, educated, industrialized, rich, and democratic. Americans are WEIRD, so are Western Europeans and Australians.

Since much psychological research is conducted among college students from WEIRD countries, the results are not necessarily representative of people from relatively less developed countries nor representative of those who are Conservative. Thus, you need to think about whether psychological research applies beyond the WEIRD countries. The Liberals who criticize capitalism are all from WEIRD capitalistic countries.

Among the few bits of research that have been done outside of the WEIRD areas, less developed cultures have higher levels of the Ethical Zone of belonging than those in the West. This is reflected in an Eastern European saying: "If you're in a position of power and you don't use it to enrich yourself, you're stealing from your family." (Credit to Brad Agle of Brigham Young University for turning me on to the saying.)

In the past few years, nativist parties that reject immigration have been rising in Eastern Europe, the dark side of the strong belonging ties in non-WEIRD countries.

Kinship in Africa is a broad concept, extending beyond the nuclear family to the children of siblings or even cousins. The title of Hillary Clinton's book *It Takes a Village* is derived from an African quote that represents the responsibility of the village in raising a child. Black South

Africans use the phrase "black tax" to describe the contribution that is expected from them to their family.

You can get a sense of the strong African society community in the best-selling series *No. 1 Ladies Detective Agency*. Even though it was written by a Scotsman, Alexander McCall captures the obligations of family clearly, as well as the strong allegiance of the people to the country of Botswana, another aspect of the belonging Ethical Zone.

The belonging Ethical Zone represents a support system that protects against sudden upsets, like injury, loss of a job, or illness. One study conducted in Kenya showed that a quarter of income for poor rural households comes from friends and family members. The belonging support system is why Conservatives in the US don't move from their rural areas.

A story illustrates what can happen when strong belonging Ethical Zones collide with Liberal values. Over a century ago, missionaries from the developed world started a hospital in western Africa. For decades, the administration of the hospital came from the organizers in the developed world. Eventually, the board decided to transition the hospital to local control. The new administrator (an African) embezzled some money. The board of directors thought that they had just made a bad choice, so they fired that person and hired a different local person as administrator. That person misused funds also!

After reading Jonathan Haidt's book *The Righteous Mind*, the board figured out what was going on. The locals were extremely high in the belonging and community Ethical Zone. When a family member needed money, they had to say yes. Their Ethical Zone of belonging was stronger than any responsibility they felt to the hospital, the patients, or the donors.

CONSOLIDATING WHAT WE HAVE LEARNED

THE BELONGING AND community Ethical Zone is the fundamental building block to understand why the political landscape is so fractured and why it sets up an emotional minefield. Belonging arises out of our evolutionary history.

As we will learn in the biology chapter, belonging affects our brain functioning, saliva production, and sweat. It is a powerful force that affects our opinions, our self-image, and even our longevity. The degree to which people belong to groups varies by political affiliation, and the decline of other affiliations has led to political affiliation becoming the dominant way of belonging and a substitute for religion.

Belonging has both positives and negatives. The sunny sides are increased happiness and life span. The dark sides of belonging are conformity and the degree to which we think of people not like us as other. Your group winning has become extremely important and leads to people avoiding objects and activities that are favored by other groups. The Ethical Zone of belonging is stronger among Conservatives and in non-WEIRD countries.

2
WHO DO YOU FOLLOW? AUTHORITY AND LEADERSHIP

I F YOU ARE wondering what authority has to do with persuasion and preaching, you might be tempted to skip this chapter. But when you take a stand that you know better than the people you are talking to, you are preaching and inherently trying to use authority.

Here's the Ethical Framework with the second Ethical Zone named:

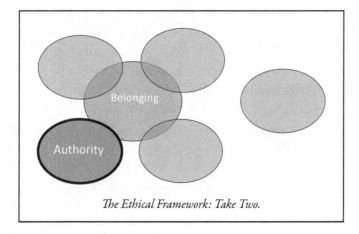

The Ethical Framework: Take Two.

Just like belonging and community, respect for authority comes out of our evolutionary history. Groups that had competent leaders survived; thus, we are all descended from them. Alan Fiske (the anthropologist who originated the relational model theory, an input into moral foundations theory) concluded that as societies increased in size and density, they transitioned from communal sharing to a stage where having an authority figure helped them organize more effectively.

Then, as the population continued to increase, respect for authority became more important in determining what is viewed as right and wrong. Historical examples of this would be a king or even the lord of the manor during feudal times. What the king said was what mattered, not whether it was true or right. Or as King Louis XIV of France said: *"L'etat c'est moi"* ("I am the state").

> *As societies increased in size and density, they transitioned from communal sharing to a stage where having an authority figure helped them organize more effectively.*

Respect for authority is also noted as a stage of Western childhood psychological development. In that stage, young children believe that right is what an authority figure said. After puberty, this research found that children age out of unquestioning acceptance of what an authority figure says.

But that research with children came out of a well-educated Western-world sensibility (as mentioned earlier—the WEIRD societies, Western educated industrial rich democracies), so that paradigm isn't true for people in smaller and less densely populated societies and other cultures.

Just like in the other Ethical Zones, there are differences within the population, both by group and individually. In the US, Conservatives tend to be higher on respect for authority. Those in Eastern Europe are higher in respect for authority and are more likely to favor authoritarian regimes. A majority of people in the world live in an authoritarian or semi-authoritarian society. This means they don't have a free press, they don't have courts that are independent, and their bank account can be confiscated.

THE PSYCHOLOGICAL UNDERPINNINGS OF AUTHORITY

IN THE PREVIOUS chapter, I talked about how all humans need to belong, that we all need community, and that politics has become the dominant group identification, and I talked about how some of those differences drive the disparity between Liberals and Conservatives. But what determines how you feel about authority?

Political science and psychological research offer several potential explanations. One relevant area of research says people differ in their need to come to a quick conclusion (called high need for cognitive closure or HNFCC) and that this is what drives political affiliation. People who have HNFCC tend to be Conservative and have high respect for authority. (Note that this has no association with intelligence! They aren't stupid, they just need to come to conclusions quickly.)

Another way to clearly identify people who are high in respect for authority is to ask questions about parenting style. The questions all start like this: "Which one is more important for a child to have?" Questions are asked in four areas:

1. Independence versus respect for elders
2. Obedience versus self-reliance
3. Curiosity versus good manners
4. Being considerate versus being well behaved

Those who answer respect, obedience, good manners, and being well behaved are more likely to have what is called a fixed mindset, which indicates a Conservative mindset and one that is high in respect for authority. This mindset comes from their worldview. Those have a worldview that the world is a scary place choose obedience-related attributes, and those whose worldview says that the world is a relatively safe place choose openness-related attributes. Thus, a fixed mindset and parenting style is one way respect for authority is transmitted to the next generation.

But these differences are probably related to the environment in which these people have been raised. People who are raised in a less affluent, less safe environment haven't had their needs met in the same way as those who were raised in a more prosperous environment. Relating this to the Maslow hierarchy of needs, not having security needs met as a child means they have higher safety needs as adults than those who did.

Importantly, these differences also relate to personality differences: Those who are high in authority tend to be low on openness to new experiences and high on conscientiousness, two of the "big five" personality traits. Research shows that societies that are low in openness are less likely to innovate.

Thus, being high in respect for authority is associated with maintaining order and control, as well as with obedience and fending off chaos. When you have an authority figure in charge, you know what to expect. Implicit in this is a responsibility that the leader has for his followers. Further, there is consistency and structure involved in this Ethical Zone.

Consistency and Truth

An example of the power that authority can have on convincing people to take action can be found in the notorious experiments that Stanley Milgram did in the 1960s. As you may remember, the Milgram experiments convinced many of its participants to give very high (potentially lethal) electric shocks to another person.

While we know in retrospect that the shocks were fake, and the so-called victim was a confederate of the actor who was posing as a researcher, the research subjects didn't know. They were influenced by a white man in an experimenter's white coat—a typical authority figure. The subjects afterward said that they went through with giving shocks even though they felt uneasy because they didn't want to let the experimenter down. They believed the experimenter wouldn't have them take an action that was really bad, and they didn't want to ruin the experiment.

This observation gives an interesting insight into authority. They trusted the authority figure to tell them the right action to do. They trusted the authority figure to tell them the truth.

Another researcher has followed up on Milgram's experiments and discovered that our brain waves are different when we are following orders than when we make a conscious choice. The Ethical Zone of respect for authority is indeed powerful.

Authority Helps People Make Sense of the World

Another part of what respect for authority does is this: You don't have to work to make sense of the world and what is true; it is done for you. It is easier to give over agency for your own life to an authority figure. It is uncomfortable to have to make your own decisions, to take responsibility for your own decisions when you might be wrong.

If that were the case, you would be to blame for what is wrong with your life. It feels more difficult to make your own choices. Doing what you are told to do may lead to more pronounced happiness (religious people are on average happier than those who are not) and lead to less anxiety (Liberals are more anxious than Conservatives).

A sentence in a 2017 job posting for a pastor wanted for a church in West Virginia illustrates some of this thinking: "We want a pastor who will tell us what to think and believe." That's a revealing statement about the respect for authority Ethical Zone. This Conservative congregation also wanted a leader who believed in the inerrancy of the Bible, so they weren't open to new beliefs (no novelty for us Conservatives!). The ad for the pastor is certainly different from what one would read for a religious congregation in my home state of New Jersey, which has more Liberals.

It's difficult to make sense of the world—the world is a chaotic place with no consistency. I realize that statement takes a Liberal point of view. A Conservative would have written that "God makes sense of this world; He is the force behind everything."

I don't want to lecture you on theology; I just want to say that if you want to persuade people, you need to be aware of that difference, which should be integrated in the way you talk to your audience. Most books on this topic are written by atheists, but they don't have the same insight that those of us who are not atheists have.

The high need for cognitive closure means that Conservatives are not open to ambiguity or nuance. They aren't going to sit still for a complicated explanation. They will go with the tried-and-true that they trust.

Implicit in this is their trust that the authority figure is telling the truth. This is their Achilles heel that makes them susceptible to fake news. It also tells you as a communicator that Liberals need more information than Conservatives. The needs of who you are talking to should determine your content.

Trust

As I just mentioned, Conservatives place a lot of trust in an authority figure. That means choosing an authority figure to trust is a major deal.

Research into trust in general has shown that truth telling, consistency, and dependability are keys to developing trust.

Because the research I reference did not segment people by political leaning, we can't say for certain that these are the factors that lead Conservatives to trust a particular authority figure, but we do know that consistency and dependability are extremely important to Conservatives. Another factor about whom to trust is probably related to the belonging Ethical Zone, that you trust the same authority figure that the others in your tribe trust.

Other elements that breed trust are respect and dealing with risk. The concept of respect is grounded in respecting relationships. It can be difficult to be respectful when your worldview is different. Lack of respect manifests as condescension and disdain. It's pretty common for Conservatives to feel that Liberals are being condescending, so Conservatives are probably unlikely to trust a Liberal.

Finally, dealing with risk refers to actions to get people involved in new activities. Change is uncomfortable for Conservatives. If you are going to get a Conservative to change their mind, it is more important to engage them in any change effort. It is also important to emphasize the ways in which the world is not changing. To develop trust, you have to help Conservatives with change.

The Rebels

The flip side of respect for authority is rebellion and anarchy. The Enlightenment and American and French revolutions (less than a century after Louis XIV said "*L'etat c'est moi*," the ultimate statement of an authority figure) represent the beginnings of the flowering of independent thought and need for self-determination. Words like *opposition, protest, refuse,* and *obstruct* capture this pushback. But it can also be a little subtler. In conversations with Liberals, I heard the same comment repeatedly: "I respect authority when it is earned/justified/deserved."

Judging whether a leader is worthy of being followed may be a relatively recent change as the opposition to authority has flourished. In his 1977 book *Servant Leadership*, Robert Greenleaf noted that respect for authority has been declining over time, noting that the campus protests and disrespect for authority arose out of antiwar protests. Those who grew up in the sixties were rebelling against authority and associated power with exploitation and evil.

This opposition has climbed since then, as documented by trend researchers at Pew. Even today young people have less trust in authority figures than their elders. The reasons for the decline cited by experts all have to do with bad behavior by the authority figures. But human nature probably hasn't changed; that behavior may be consistent with that of earlier rulers. Instead, what is most likely happening is a product of rising expectations of authority figures, because of the more optimistic worldview. The optimists become disappointed because they expect more.

The Volkswagen Beetle and its iconic "Think Small" ad provides a noteworthy example of a product that appealed to those who were rebelling (read: younger and low in respect for authority) and repelled those who were high in authority (read: Conservatives and older people) who would be attracted to big and powerful cars. Both the ad and the car say, "I am rejecting your values of respecting authority."

The sixties were only the start of this rebellion. The phrase "Speak Truth to Power" represents the current manifestation of this belief.

When searching online for ads in this theme, I found an ad for LGBTQ travel that took an iconic monument (Mount Rushmore) and showed their backsides—clearly a rebellious ad that is low in respect for authority.

But even those who rebel have leaders. The Black Panther movement had Bobby Seale and Huey Newton. The antivaccine movement has leaders such as Gwyneth Paltrow and Jenny McCarthy. Black Lives Matter has leaders. Due to the higher degree of desire for novelty among the left, there is probably less attachment to individual leaders than among the right, and they have less ability to get people to work together, but they still do have leaders who are influential.

The Occupy Wall Street movement was perhaps less successful in coalescing into a long-term movement because they attempted to work without leaders out of extremely low respect for authority. Authority has value; anarchy makes it more difficult to achieve goals. Occupy may also have fallen apart because it was powered by a common enemy belonging (the enemy being the 1 percent), which isn't as strong a unifying force as real belonging, as mentioned earlier.

A leader isn't a leader unless he or she has followers, and there needs to be a match between the followers and the leader. But leaders work only because of followers; they are mutually dependent.

But how does a leader lead when people are low in respect for authority? It's tricky. As we just saw, those who study leadership have concluded effective leaders today don't have to deal only with the traditional items of tasks and relationships, they also have to deal with change.

Transparency is often viewed as the antidote to leaders who can't be trusted by those who are low in respect for authority. In my view it doesn't increase trust or respect but is viewed as a check on unbridled power. Thus, theoretically, transparency would be more important to Liberals than Conservatives.

This is a hypothesis, and I would love to see a test of this. It may also be a factor in declining trust in authority figures because no one is ever perfect and can't live up to an artificial standard. I will discuss transparency in more detail in the chapter on sacredness/purity.

PATRIARCHY AS AUTHORITY

As I HAVE been writing this book, I have been acutely aware of pronouns. Power in Western society is now and has in the past been held by men, usually white men. This is described by academia and the left as patriarchy. Thus, ads that feature an older white male (such as Dr. Marcus Welby, who also had the doctor status, which enhances his authority) appeal most to those who are high in respect for authority, such as Conservatives.

In contrast, the left views the power being held by men (and white men specifically) as illegitimate, purely an artifact of the past, reinforcing and justifying their low respect for authority perceptions. The #MeToo movement has pointed out the way that some men exploited their power and authority, as has the ongoing Catholic priest sex abuse scandals.

These are abuses of power, betraying the responsibility a leader has to his followers. These abuses of power have caused damage to untold numbers of people.

At the sentencing hearing of only one abuser (Larry Nassar who abused girls who were training in gymnastics as young as age five), stories from 155 different girls and women were heard over seven days of testimony about the ongoing negative effects of this abuse. The stories are heartbreaking and are only being heard because of the declining respect for authority in our culture. The victims' stories help us to understand the damage that abuses of power cause.

Abusive men get away with betraying the trust of those who depend on them because of the beliefs that we have about authority, which are hardwired into our thinking because we have been trained this way. It's extremely difficult to unwire them. That explains why women who are otherwise competent and effective may react in an uncharacteristically passive manner, acquiescing to abusive behavior. In the heat of the moment, people may allow activities that they are uncomfortable with because they are obeying their underlying respect for authority that they learned when they were very young.

In her TED Talk on how to overcome biases, Vernā Myers, a female diversity expert, confessed momentary uneasiness during turbulence on a flight when a female pilot made an announcement. It's amazing that even someone aware of ingrained biases still has some deep-seated beliefs in the higher competence of men and feels safer with a man in charge, even if only for a second. Interestingly, the opposite was probably true. Because women have to try harder than men and tend to take fewer risks, the female pilot actually might be a better and safer pilot.

These beliefs about authority figures also created concerns that allowing women to serve in combat roles would degrade military readiness, cohesion, and morale. Despite these concerns, women are allowed to serve with no effect on morale, cohesion, or readiness.

It remains to be seen if recent awareness of abuses by men in power and the positive experiences of competent women in male-dominated roles will result in a shift in attitudes beyond the progressive left. On the Liberal side, note that many of the authority figures of the antivaccine movement are women. Messages delivered by women and minorities are going to be more attractive to Liberal viewers than to Conservatives. Unfortunately, race also matters, which will be discussed in more detail in the sacredness chapter.

Money and Power and Authority

Money and wealth are key signifiers of authority. People with money have more power. Having a higher salary as a CEO, dictator, or preacher can act to bolster authority and is one reason why people seek money (beyond craving what it can buy). Conservatives are less likely to be against people earning lots of money and may actually view with pride how well-off those in authority are because they believe it reflects well on them that their leader is successful.

On the other hand, those on the left are more likely to be upset about high pay because, to them, the Ethical Zone of fairness is higher in importance than respect for authority. (I'll discuss this more in the chapter on fairness.)

Speaking of money, it's not surprising that those with high need for cognitive closure (read: Conservatives) are less likely to make changes to their investments such as rebalancing, as is recommended. They stick with what they believe! Only those who have hired a financial advisor (an authority) have rebalanced their portfolios, which has been shown to lead to better financial results. Thus, high respect for authority helps Conservatives to overcome some of the limitations of their HNFCC thinking style.

Companies Represent Authority

As behemoths, companies wield a lot of power. They represent authority. When they withhold relevant information, twist the truth, and outright lie, that contributes to the decline in trust in authority figures.

Tobacco companies lying about the harms caused by cigarettes, dumping of industrial waste in places like the Love Canal, pharmaceutical companies only reporting positive data on their drugs and selling opioids with misleading advertising all add to this phenomenon. Hollywood cements this mistrust of large companies with films like *The China Syndrome* and *Silkwood*.

The latest actors in this story are the financial firms whose actions aided in the Great Recession, for which no one went to jail. This mistrust is higher among Liberals, who are predisposed to believe that the economic system is rigged against individuals. When I talk to Liberals who have invested time and money in degrees that would be valued by the pharmaceutical industry where I used to work, they recoil in horror when I suggest a job in their field at a drug company.

Because companies are so large and have lots of lawyers, fear is also involved. Being sued by a large company makes people afraid. A recent news story about hospitals suing people who didn't pay their bills high-lighted the fear felt by the former patient. Noncompete clauses in employment contracts result in less mobility and fewer employment options for workers due to the fear they inspire. When I left my job at Merck and was thinking about blogging about my experience, I felt I had to choose my words very carefully so I wouldn't be sued for revealing anything I shouldn't.

Revisiting Earlier Examples

I promised to come back to the three brands, Nike, Dick's, and Gillette, to look at how respect for authority contributed to the explosive situations they faced:

- In taking a knee during the national anthem, Colin Kaepernick (and the other players, and Nike by extension) was defying the owners, mostly white men, who represent authority. Then, President Trump weighed in, suggesting that the NFL create a policy that would basically fire any player who took a knee. With the president making comments, that gives the issue increased weight for Conservatives. That's a double violation of the Ethical Zone of respect for authority. This operates in opposite ways for the two choirs: It reinforces the negative beliefs of those who are low in respect for authority and angers those who are high in respect for authority.
- The reaction to Dick's Sporting Goods not selling assault rifles could have been quieted by an authority figure, which could have happened if President Trump had come out in support of Dick's or of gun control, but he didn't. President Trump has the support of the NRA, so the explosive situation that Dick's wandered into doesn't have that Ethical Zone behind it.
- On the other hand, the Gillette #ToxicMasculinity video definitely violated the Ethical Zone of respect for authority. The campaign challenges the implied respect that men (especially Conservative men) feel they are due. The belonging and community and respect for authority Ethical Zones

reinforce each other to inflame passions against this commercial even more. This works in opposite directions for the two choirs, with Liberals believing that the assumptions behind the patriarchy should be questioned.

There's more analysis of these brands coming in the next chapter so you can more fully understand how each of the various Ethical Zones contributes to our culture wars.

Cultural Differences

To give you a flavor of some of the differences culturally, Germans and Japanese are both higher in respect for authority than people in the US and the UK. African countries are also higher, which may explain their tendency to allow strongmen to come to power.

The 2018 election of the autocratic new Brazilian president, Jair Bolsonaro, is another case of this Ethical Zone at work as is the election of Hungarian Prime Minister Victor Orban. Both have fed on the incipient nationalism in their countries, illustrating how these two Ethical Zones work together. Any campaign that is intended to be used globally needs to consider the variations in the importance of the various Ethical Zones and how they are interpreted in various cultures.

CONSOLIDATING WHAT WE LEARNED

JUST LIKE BELONGING and community, respect for authority is an evolutionarily important zone of human experience. A high level of respect for authority tends to be associated with desire for order and conscientiousness, two of the five key variables of personality, a high need for cognitive closure, and a gloomy worldview, which plays out in how people parent.

Those with high levels of respect for authority also are resistant to change (a key element of being Conservative); those who have lower levels have a high desire for novelty. The rebelliousness of the 1960s has relaxed respect for authority, although some people (especially Conservatives in the US) still have high levels.

Patriarchy is a key part of respect for authority, and empowering those who are disadvantaged may be perceived as challenging the power of patriarchy/authority, which can backfire if the group you want to convince is Conservative.

A key element of companies is that they do hold authority, but their misuse of that authority has contributed to mistrust especially among Liberals. Liberals' more optimistic worldview has given them higher expectations, which are then violated, leading to lower respect. Transparency is viewed as an antidote to untrustworthy leaders among those who are low in respect for authority, but it does not lead to increased trust. Instead, it undermines trust.

3

WHAT IS IMPORTANT: SACREDNESS, PURITY, AND DISGUST

W HAT DO ALL these ads have in common?

- A Mike's Hard Lemonade ad showing an industrial accident, with a large metal object protruding from a man's body
- A Coors Light commercial showing "hot chicks running around at parties"
- A feminine hygiene ad
- A toilet paper commercial with a bear using the product
- A man opening a beer bottle with his butt

The answer is that the five ads were all rated as disgusting by college students, who are typically Liberals.

The third of the five Ethical Zones is that of sacredness. I've added the label to the third bubble in the Ethical Framework.

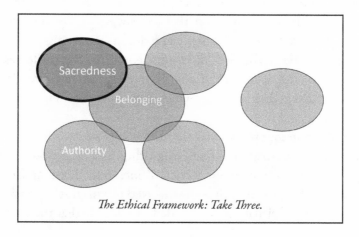

The Ethical Framework: Take Three.

Just like belonging and authority, sacredness developed from our evolutionary history. Having food that is safe to eat (not poisonous, not contaminated) was key to survival. Societies that survived developed ways to identify those foods that were safe and unsafe; we are all descended from them. (Do you see a theme? So far, all three of the Ethical Zones we have talked about have been part of our evolutionary history. We need to appreciate what these zones did for us.)

DISGUST AS AN INDICATOR OF VIOLATION

THE PHYSIOLOGICAL MECHANISM that developed to distinguish which foods were safe was disgust. Disgust is one of the basic emotions found in all cultures. It evokes the physical response of nausea. The signature disgust look was described centuries ago by Charles Darwin as having three elements: a gaping mouth with an upper lip retraction and a nose wrinkle. Neurological research demonstrates that the region of the brain that is activated by disgust is the anterior insula.

Having a physical aversion to substances that might kill you also helps you survive. Part of this survival mechanism is cleanliness. "Cleanliness is next to Godliness" captures one element of the sacredness zone. Thus, cleaning products belong in this zone. Personally, I am relatively low in this Ethical Zone, so it took me a while to figure out that the word *filth* to describe conditions that were messy, but not literally dirty, is a tip-off that the other person was operating out of the sacredness Ethical Zone.

In addition to having safe food, most societies developed some concept of the sacred, of God, or of a Higher Power. To explain why various cultures have this idea in common, theorists suggest that we humans automatically perceive a "hierarchy of social space," with the higher levels representing moral purity, or God, then animals, and, finally, the lowest levels of depravity or the devil. Evolutionarily, having a shared concept of the Divine bound together societies, which may have also helped them survive.

What ties together these ideas are the feelings we get when sacredness norms are violated, disgust. "That's disgusting" is a clear tip-off that you are operating in the sacredness Ethical Zone, even if you aren't talking about food. In fact, the mouth being involved in a disgust expression even in nonfood-related situations is regarded as evidence that the emotion of disgust originated out of the need to avoid contaminated foods and poisons.

Another theorist suggests that disgust may also signal that community-defining norms are being violated. Ideas that help promote group cohesion were to be prized, and ideas that threaten the group were to be abhorred. Regardless of why or how disgust occurs, academic research has confirmed that inhibiting nausea with ginger reduces the *moral* disgust reaction. (More about this later.)

One hallmark of disgust is the idea it might spread, using words such as *contamination*, *viral*, or *epidemic*. There's an element of danger about lack of sacredness, a lack of safety. This is reminiscent of the safety need from Maslow's hierarchy of needs.

> *There's an element of danger about lack of sacredness, a lack of safety.*

Examples of the Sacredness Ethical Zone

What makes the Ethical Zone of sacredness confusing is that different societies and cultures place different interpretations on this zone. Disgust is defined by culture. In the US, Conservatives and Liberals react very differently based on what they believe is sacred.

You can see by the examples of Liberal sacredness cited at the beginning of the chapter that what the college kids held as sacred was treating all people well and perhaps treating the disadvantaged as sacred (this will be discussed further in the next chapter).

Opposition to the death penalty because life is sacred is a way of talking about this Ethical Zone among Liberals. Calling a certain way of eating "clean" taps into this zone among Liberals. "Eat Clean Bro" is an "all-natural prepared meal" kit service.

The phrase "Clean Plate" is used as a restaurant name that invokes this Ethical Zone, as does *clean* in a brand name for a cleaning product and when a website uses the promotional line: "Find healthy food, delicious recipes, nutrition news, and wellness tips at Clean Plates, plus great new food products and restaurants for clean eating." Organic food is viewed as pure (which means sacred). A vegetarian sausage company that has branded itself "No evil" is also drawing on this Ethical Zone.

Liberals view foods made with GMOs as disgusting. I once heard someone say GMO food isn't real food. In fact, a study of people who were strongly opposed to GMOs showed a disgust response from imagining eating a genetically modified item. Yellow rice, which has been genetically modified to provide beta-carotene for malnourished people in developing countries, has not been distributed because of the GMO sacredness Ethical Zone issue.

Besides food, this Ethical Zone influences health decisions. Research has demonstrated that antivaccine attitudes are stronger among mothers who are high in sacredness, even among Liberals.

On the other side, Conservatives hold as sacred religion, marriage, families, chastity, scripture, and certain music. The phrase "body is a temple" illustrates the right's emphasis. An ad for an abortion clinic would qualify as disgusting for Conservatives. An ad campaign for a Merck vaccine for HPV (which said that parents have an obligation to protect their children against cancer caused by sexually transmitted diseases) has been called disgusting, presumably among the right because of its implication of lack of sex purity.

I haven't found a list of ads that the right finds disgusting, but one published study mentioned that even impure thoughts can cause disgust among those who are religious. While there is a lot of individual variability among people, Conservatives in general have higher sensitivity to disgust.

DOMAINS OF DISGUST

MANY PRODUCTS WE use fall in the sacredness zone, either in the positive or negative. The domains of disgust described by Rozin and Haidt are these:

- Food products
- Body-related products
- Animals
- Sexual activities (including homosexuality)

- Death, illness, or corpses
- Exterior body violations (such as rashes, gashes, blemishes, and deformity)
- Poor hygiene and cleanliness
- Social order violations that can elicit moral disgust (example: cheating)

Thus, companies that sell food, scents, cleaning products, and bodily waste categories are operating in this Ethical Zone. Drugs for disfiguring diseases are also, as are the opposite: beauty products. While advertisers in these categories have learned to navigate this Ethical Zone, they can still make mistakes, such as the toilet paper bear commercial on the college students' hate list.

Food illness outbreaks, such as the ones experienced at Chipotle in 2015 and 2016, awaken our disgust reflex. Although some may think that showing the actual ingredients may be a way of reassuring people, one academic study demonstrated that showing raw meat awakens the disgust reflex. That doesn't seem to be the answer. To address the sacredness Ethical Zone, some food companies have developed codes that provide information on where the food was sourced, which shows a use of transparency.

The trend toward crystals reflects the use of the sacredness Ethical Zone. Urban Outfitters sells four different types of crystal clusters. Besides the use of crystals as healing modalities and as sacred objects, they are being incorporated into marketing and actual products for women: Sephora and Estée Lauder are using gemstone terminology, and Sephora is offering a pearl mask and rose quartz luminizer.

Other Ways Sacredness Is Used

There are signature colors for sacredness. A search for pure images on Google resulted in pictures of white roses, clear blue water, and women in white bridal dresses. There's a reason why Mr. Clean's clothes stay white as he cleans. White is the color of sacredness and purity—think bridal dresses and Ivory soap that is "99% pure." Nivea tied their brand to this Ethical Zone when it used the line "white is purity."

Similarly, when I did a test of colors for an asthma inhaler, white was the color with the highest ratings for safety—connoting a lack of dangerousness. Blue was next (both colors that relate to this zone). Transparency can also indicate purity; Neutrogena soap that is so clear you can see through it connotes this Ethical Zone as did Johnson & Johnson's decision to take the yellow color out of its baby shampoo. Clear plastic egg cartons also evoke purity.

I once did market research on a powerful ad that illustrated intense pain by superimposing a pattern of shattered glass over a knee. That image made people so uncomfortable that the brand manager toned it down by changing the color of the shattered-glass pattern from red to blue. The implied violation of the skin tapped into the sacredness Ethical Zone, and the blue color softened the impact because it counteracted the implied violation.

An ad can inadvertently touch the sacredness Ethical Zone in other ways, such as using women in an objectifying way, which provokes outrage from Liberals as an interpersonal offense. A Pinterest page devoted to disgusting ads includes ads with human and animal waste and ads that use women in sexist and demeaning ways.

In the previously mentioned study that asked college students to identify two ads that they found disgusting, the major categories were these: "gross" depictions (such as the metal object protruding from a man's body) as well as ads that were "indecent, sexually oriented, sexist and sexually objectifying portrayals," such as the Coors beer hot chicks ad mentioned in the opening of this chapter.

A recent IKEA ad that offered a discount on cribs for pregnant women if they urinated on the print ad (to reveal the discount) may have also provoked a disgust response, especially among those who are high in purity.

Unfortunately, it seems that fat people also violate societal standards and the sacredness Ethical Zone. The Pinterest page of disgusting ads had several pictures of fat people, with excess flesh bulging out. Dove's device of using real women who don't meet the societal standards of being anorexically thin would probably appeal more to those who are low in the sacredness zone.

Nonprofits use disgust in ads relatively often. An academic study on the effectiveness of using disgust in advertising used images from the Montana Meth Project, an award-winning campaign that uses images such as a teenager with open sores on his face. When reviewing ad compendiums on the internet, I found an ad from the nonprofit World Wildlife Fund of a woman pulling a suitcase through the airport leaving a trail of blood, with the headline, "Don't buy exotic animal souvenirs."

Safety

As I just mentioned, because danger is the opposite of sacredness, safety becomes a dimension of this zone. But experts note that lack of *perceived* safety is not *actual* danger. The cues we use to determine safety come from the sacredness dimension and are not an accurate reflection of danger.

The media adversely affect our sense of safety because they amplify our sense of being threatened in order to get attention. The news plays on a psychological phenomenon called the availability heuristic. In other words, because we can think about the news articles we have read, the items we have read about become more real to us. Except they really aren't.

Examples of this contradiction between perception and reality abound. Sharks have killed fewer people than tornados and sinkholes, but who knows this? And what do we fear more? Sharks. Our awareness of crime has increased, even as crime rates have declined. Almost by definition, if an item is newsworthy, it isn't worth being afraid of.

Another example is nuclear power, which is perceived as unsafe. Because nuclear disasters get a lot of press coverage, these episodes create fear, but the actual death toll from nuclear power disasters is much lower than the number of people killed from the pollution caused by burning fossil fuels. Vaccines are perceived as more dangerous than the diseases they prevent when the opposite is true.

We also get tripped up by the items we like. What we like is viewed as safer than what we dislike.

The antidotes are transparency and rationality. I will consider rationality more fully in the chapter devoted to it, but let's dig into the idea of transparency now.

Transparency

Transparency is a huge topic, which I will just touch on lightly here. It could be a book of its own.

In politics, transparency is viewed as an antidote to corruption of bad leadership and is part of the sacredness Ethical Zone among Liberals. The emphasis in the Federal Election Commission has been to require that whoever pays for an ad has to identify themselves ("My name is xxx, and I approve this message.").

The Russian meddling in the 2016 election is viewed as egregious breach of trust by those who care about transparency. But I heard one Conservative say, who cares? This may just be a reflection of the gloomy worldview of Conservatives, but I have also heard some say what difference does it make if you agree with the message anyway. No one wants to believe that they are being manipulated.

It's no surprise that one of the first actions of an autocratic ruler is to shut down the free press. The decline of local newspapers in the US is believed to have contributed to amplified local corruption. Increased transparency appears to reduce corruption.

Transparency puts the burden of weeding through the information and making a decision on the reader and not on the expert or authority. The terms of service on websites that we all speed through without reading are a prime example of the downsides of transparency. As one person who was shown the data that his phone collected that he didn't realize said: "Whenever you agree to an app, there's those eight pages of two-point font to read and, yeah, I'm guilty of not reading—just hit accept and roll the dice."

People have chosen to be transparent about their lives on social media. Posting the meals you are eating, the restaurants where you are eating, the trips you are taking makes tracking someone's life much easier. But on social media, we choose the best to post. We curate our life and don't post our troubles, which leads to a distorted picture of our lives. Our transparent life is not our actual life. As Byung-Chul Han, a South Korean–born German philosopher, has stated, transparency is not the same as truth.

The internet has made many facts transparent that used to be able to be hidden. No longer can people lie with impunity about their backgrounds, because if you check Facebook or LinkedIn, you can find out the truth. Pruning the first job or the date you graduated from college off the resume for old people to avoid agism isn't useful any longer. It doesn't matter; Google has your age on the first page of search results on your name.

Transparency may not accomplish what we think it will. Despite the belief that knowing information will make us feel safer, the opposite can occur. In fact, because life is not perfect, transparency can actually heighten the sense of danger. As I mentioned earlier, showing raw food could be interpreted as being transparent, but it awakens the disgust reflex.

Uber tried to provide transparency with a report on violence, but it didn't make people feel safer riding with their drivers. Even though the numbers were low when put into context, the report was called "highly alarming" by a criminologist.

This pattern was repeated with a report from Airbnb. The horror stories of guests having parties that result in violence overshadow the huge number of uneventful rentals. The scientific community tried to get over the issues raised about GMOs by being transparent about what they are doing on the new technology of gene drives, but activists were still suspicious.

I will repeat myself, transparency doesn't increase trust among people who have low trust to start with. Trust has been broken between authority figures and Liberals; transparency won't fix it.

PREJUDICE AND SACREDNESS

THERE'S AN ELEPHANT in this chapter that I need to address: the issue of the "other," racial and sexual prejudice issues. This is a touchy subject, so I will try my best not to offend anyone, but this is difficult, so please read with kind eyes. I am not saying that this is right; I am describing what the research says. Don't shoot me, I'm just the messenger.

The sacredness zone is a contributing factor to racial and sexual prejudice. Other zones may be involved (especially the othering that was referenced in the chapter on belonging and community). The tip-off that tells you which Ethical Zone is involved can be found in the language being used.

When the Nazis used the words *racial purity*, they were invoking the sacredness zone. When immigrants are called "animals" who are "infesting" the rest of the country, the person was operating in the sacredness Ethical Zone. In the scandal about police officers who have been sharing comments about migrants in a private group on Facebook, including calling Muslims "goat-humpers" and "savages," they were using violations of this Ethical Zone.

When women in some societies are considered unclean when they are menstruating (in some developing countries women must leave their house during menstruation), this is the sacredness zone. The disgusted reaction to the feminine hygiene ad by the college students mentioned early in the chapter is the developed-world equivalent to the menstruating women issue.

The US history of slavery was justified based on bogus reasoning that slaves were less than fully human (note that this means they are lower on the sacredness scale). The previously mentioned Nivea ad with the tagline "white is purity" referring to its product was appropriated by some hate groups for use because of the prejudice associated with this Ethical Zone. Because Nivea was only thinking about its product, and not about the other aspects of this Ethical Zone, the company probably didn't even think that the ad could be interpreted differently.

Regardless of Nivea's original intent, because this Ethical Zone does encompass race, some people on the right took advantage of Nivea's ad. I say those on the right because Conservatives are more sensitive to race. Images of people of another race are more likely to be perceived as threatening than those of the same race. This reflects their sacredness Ethical Zone.

These reactions have a deep origin and may, in fact, be innate. Psychologists have done studies with young children (as young as six months) to see where they spend more time gazing, and they spend more time looking at pictures of people that are like the ones they see every day, people of the same race. (Note: If children are raised by caregivers of a different race before age eight, their brains act as though they were of the race of the caregiver. If they join the different-race caregivers after age eight, they don't.) The researchers who did the study of infant gazing interpret it to mean that, as humans, we have innate preferences for those who are like us.

This finding may partially explain what is involved in the sacredness Ethical Zone. Another study among adults showed that different areas of our brain are engaged when we see someone of the same race versus someone of a different race. But studies also find that as people become more educated and more exposed to others who are different in a positive way, those prejudices start to erode.

Those who have college educations are lower in the sacredness Ethical Zone than those who have less education. They are using both their rational brains and another Ethical Zone (discussed in the next chapter) to overcome what may be an innate human preference for people like ourselves. In fact, they have overcome it to such an extent that a recent study found that young white Liberals actually have a slight preference for those who are of another race.

In general, because Conservatives are higher in both the sacredness and the belonging Ethical Zones, they are more likely to be higher in racial prejudice. There has been a trend to show mixed racial groupings in advertising, which may be received differently by people with different sensitivities to the sacredness zone. Liberals will be more positive toward this, while Conservatives may not be.

This doesn't mean that *all* Liberals and Conservatives are this way, because there is wide variability in the dispersion of the zones. For example, someone I know who is very high on the sacredness zone calls himself "left of Michael Moore." Similarly, many antivaccine advocates who are high in the Ethical Zone of sacredness are Liberals.

Again, these aren't my attitudes. I do not believe the prejudice associated with this Ethical Zone is acceptable. I personally have been working to vanquish my own bias. I am only describing what the research says.

You may be tempted to continue to preach or rail against those who are prejudiced, but this Ethical Zone and its psychological and biological underpinnings are part of why preaching doesn't work. But don't get discouraged. Even though you can't change people's prejudice, you can change people's minds about specific issues. Be sure to check out the reframing chapter for details.

Finally, it may be that this part of the Ethical Zone is flexible and can encompass other ideas. It may be that democracy or liberty is viewed as sacred. Lots of research could be done in this area. It is important for you to know how this concept touches your product space.

Revisiting Earlier Examples

You can probably see that the sacredness Ethical Zone is involved in

Nike's Colin Kaepernick issue just because it is about black men—both those who are taking a knee during the national anthem and the black men who are being killed.

The Parkland shooting/Dick's Sporting Goods gun-control issue is slightly different. So far, I've just discussed the belonging and community Ethical Zone. But I wonder if guns have taken on a mythical importance among Conservatives and whether guns themselves have moved into the sacredness Ethical Zone. That would certainly help to explain why the emotions run so high among Conservatives about this issue. This is an issue worth researching.

The combination of more than one Ethical Zone yields a more powerful connection.

Cultural Differences

This chapter has focused on WEIRD North American culture and how it experiences sacredness and disgust. While much of the literature that discusses this has been done in English-speaking countries, all societies experience this Ethical Zone, but differently. In India, the Ethical Zone of sacredness affects perceptions of those of different castes and represents a virtue to be protected, even by murder.

In Japan, as in North America, corruption violates the social order and is regarded as "dirty"—another tip-off that the Ethical Zone is sacredness. The antidote to corruption is believed to be transparency, which fits in with the sacredness Ethical Zone. Homophobia in Africa and other developing nations reflects the expanded importance they place on this Ethical Zone, more than we do in the rich world. This is discussed further in Part II.

If you want to be effective in persuading those outside the WEIRD world, you need to understand the sacredness Ethical Zone in order to avoid transgressing the culturally based sacredness norms of the society.

CONSOLIDATING WHAT WE HAVE LEARNED

THE THIRD ETHICAL Zone has evolutionary history of sacredness, purity, and disgustingness. This zone touches off different reactions in our brains and even manifests in how long infants stare at pictures of others. This zone derives evolutionarily from being able to discern safe food, and the signature expression of disgust indicating violation of this Ethical Zone is a curled upper lip. This reaction has been generalized to animals, waste products, violating the body's boundaries, and even more broadly to those who violate society's moral code. There are certain words that help you discern when this Ethical Zone is being invoked.

Like the first two zones, this zone is stronger among Conservatives, but there are manifestations among Liberals as seen in the antivaccine movement and in "clean" food.

Importantly, this Ethical Zone is also the source of prejudice, which is signaled by language of infestation or infecting or dirty. Other cultures have the same zone; the interpretation varies, but the underlying concept is the same. Violating more than one Ethical Zone makes the issue even more powerful, as illustrated by the analysis of the underlying factors behind the reactions to the Nike, Dick's, and Gillette issues.

Transparency is part of this Ethical Zone. While it does appear to rein in corruption, it may not increase trust.

4
WHO GETS REWARDED?
FAIRNESS AND MERIT

"It's not fair!"

Kids have a finely developed sense of fairness, but it may not be what parents want to hear. A search of titles at a local library turned up several books for parents to use to teach their children about fairness, but almost none for adults. The theme of the books is how children should share.

Books on fairness aren't needed. Psychological research among young children (as young as three years old) demonstrates that children develop a sense of what is fair very early. For kids, research has shown that what is fair has two parts to it: equal shares when effort isn't involved (equality), and proportionate shares when effort is involved (merit). This is the fourth Ethical Zone: fairness.

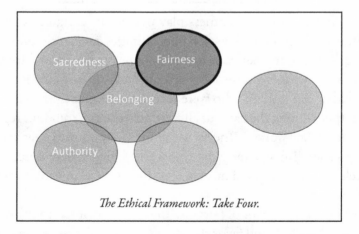

The Ethical Framework: Take Four.

As adults, when we think about the fairness Ethical Zone, we each prefer one flavor. Conservatives place more emphasis on merit, while Liberals place more emphasis on equality. We usually only think about the one we prefer, not the other flavor of fairness that kids have instinctively.

Because adults concentrate on one flavor of fairness and don't recognize the other flavors, and because we use the same word but actually have different concepts, the Ethical Zone of fairness has become a source of major conflict in the United States. When someone says they are concerned about income inequality, the chances are high that they are a Liberal because that is about equality.

In fact, because the most Liberal among us recognize historical inequality and because they are extremely high on the Ethical Zone of care/harm, they sometimes favor giving more shares to those who are disadvantaged to make up for previous inequities. The interaction of these factors leads to a third flavor of fairness: need.

> *Because adults concentrate on one flavor of fairness and don't recognize the other flavors, and because we use the same word but actually have different concepts, the Ethical Zone of fairness has become a source of major conflict in the United States.*

These different flavors of fairness play out in our disagreements about healthcare, college admissions, job opportunities, and arrests and jail sentencing. This conflict between the two dominant flavors of fairness isn't new; it is at least as old as the New Testament. It can be found in the story Jesus told of the workers who were recruited to work in the vineyard at various times during the day, but all were paid the same amount regardless of how long they worked. The owner of the vineyard paid equality wages (all the same). The workers who had worked longer were upset because they felt they had deserved more wages than those who hadn't worked as long as they had.

That's the merit flavor of fairness. The irony is that Conservatives who are more biblically based favor the merit flavor of fairness, while Jesus was advocating the equality flavor of fairness.

The paradox is that equality and need-based flavors of fairness have developed only in capitalist economies, not in the socialist economies that were imposed, such as in China and the former Soviet Union.

Because Liberals favor the equality flavor of fairness, they are likely to feel that the economy is unfair more than Conservatives do.

Note that in this conversation we are always talking about comparisons. Our brain seems to be hardwired to compare ourselves to others. The rational counterargument to the Liberal point of view is the fact that prosperity has increased overall in the world and fewer people are hungry. But this rational argument doesn't matter when your lens is the *comparative* well-being.

The fairness Ethical Zone interacts with the belonging Ethical Zone. Those who have more of a merit flavor to their fairness Ethical Zone will also believe that those in their in-group also deserve more. This element binds groups together (and it is helpful for groups to be bound together. Really! That's the positive side of belonging).

HOW COMPANIES USE FAIRNESS

THESE CONCEPTS ARE used by companies in advertising occasionally. It's not a major theme, but ads that use the terms *deserve* or *worth it* are invoking the fairness zone. One observer believes that two campaigns were behind the trend to use fairness: the McDonald's "You Deserve a Break Today" campaign and the L'Oréal "You Are Worth It" campaign. This has led to other advertisers picking up on this theme and, some say, contributing to a shift to an entitlement culture.

This Ethical Zone is invoked ever so lightly when retailers provide benefits to their frequent customers, or to those who have loyalty cards. When a store requires that customers buy a certain combination of purchases or requires them to sign in before they get a discount, they are saying (implicitly) you have to work to get a special deal. That's the merit flavor of fairness.

Pricing is also another area where fairness is invoked. An ad for WaWa Convenience Stores, which promotes that all sizes of coffee are the same price, is using the equality flavor of fairness. When Walmart charges "everyday low prices," they are in the equality-flavored fairness Ethical Zone. Other stores that vary the prices whether you are part of their loyalty program or have purchased a certain number of items (both relating to earning the discount, either by participation in a group or an achievement) are using the merit flavor Ethical Zone.

Some drug manufacturers price their drugs so that all dosage strengths are priced the same, while others make it proportionate to the amount of drug in the pill, reflecting the two major flavors of fairness.

Theoretically, I would expect Liberals to be more in favor of Walmart's pricing system, and Conservatives to back the store loyalty program discounts, but I don't see any rhetoric to that effect. Instead, other Ethical Zones override the fairness-related pricing perceptions. Perhaps putting more emphasis on the equality flavor of Walmart's pricing could begin to make Liberals feel more positively toward the retailer.

Large price increases violate our sense of fairness because they aren't based on either equality or merit. A store that raises the price of plywood after a hurricane or a gas station that hikes the price of gas during a shortage are the targets of rage.

Pharma exec (and now convicted felon) Martin Shkreli's price increase for Daraprim (a drug to treat a rare disease) generated ire both because it was such a large price increase (violating Conservatives' desire for consistency and order) and also because it was undeserved (violating Liberals' sense of fairness). Shkreli didn't do anything except use his shareholders' money to buy the drug; he didn't invent the drug or do clinical trials to test the drug, he just bought it.

Branded pharmaceutical companies who have spent years of effort and millions of dollars to develop new drugs still get pushback for their high prices, but nowhere near the outrage directed at Shkreli, perhaps because the *effort* behind the branded drugs at least somewhat justifies the high price (the merit flavor of fairness).

The New York City Marathon has incorporated the various flavors of fairness in the various ways they offer runners to qualify for the race. If you want to race in the NY Marathon, you can apply to be included in a random drawing (the equality-based flavor of fairness), or you can qualify by running faster times (the merit-based flavor of fairness), or you can raise money for charity (a different form of merit-based fairness), or you can participate in several local races and volunteering (a merging of the belonging Ethical Zone with fairness).

CONSOLIDATING WHAT WE HAVE LEARNED

THE FAIRNESS ETHICAL Zone has two main flavors: equality and merit. These appear to be instinctual, as demonstrated by research among very young children. Although we all have them both, as we come of age, we come to place more of an emphasis on one or the other.

Conservatives favor the merit flavor, while Liberals favor the equality flavor. Another flavor of fairness is becoming more popular among those on the political far left—that of making it up to those who haven't been treated equally or have bigger needs.

Conflicts arise when we don't recognize that the flavor of the fairness Ethical Zone being used is different than our own. This Ethical Zone has been used in pricing of products and when we require people to take an action to qualify for a benefit or discount, such as quantity or loyalty discounts. This Ethical Zone is also behind the outrage consumers feel for large price increases.

5

WHEN HEARTS EXPLODE: CARE/HARM

"IF IT BLEEDS, it leads."

This phrase isn't just about violence; it refers to stories that tug on your heartstrings. Newspaper articles and television news in Liberal media regularly activate our Ethical Zone of care/harm, because they know that those articles and segments get more attention and evoke more emotion.

Now that I know this, I have started to feel manipulated, so it doesn't work as well on me as it used to. This Ethical Zone is why statistics aren't as compelling as faces of those affected; statistics don't arouse our care/harm Ethical Zone. Activating the care/harm Ethical Zone causes our hearts to explode.

This is the fifth Ethical Zone, care/harm, which I have added to the Ethical Framework:

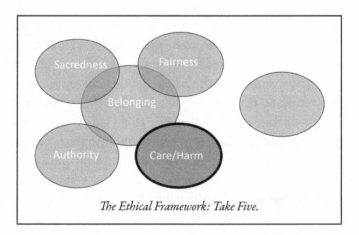

The Ethical Framework: Take Five.

The importance placed on the care/harm Ethical Zone has grown as societies have become wealthier and more developed. Liberals place much more importance on the care/harm Ethical Zone. Children who are raised in Conservative families that are comfortable may develop more of an emphasis on care/harm than their parents have because of the sunnier worldview that people develop when their world is stable. This is part of a long-term trend of movement toward people becoming more Liberal, but since the Great Recession began in 2008, this trend may have reversed.

EMPATHY: THE BASIS OF THE CARE/HARM ETHICAL ZONE

THE CARE/HARM ETHICAL Zone is based on humans' inborn tendency for empathy. One of the ways to study empathy and the lack of it is to look at those who lack it: psychopaths. Brain scans of criminal psychopaths show that they lack normal activity in regions of the brain that are now recognized to be the seat of empathy (the amygdala). Psychologists who study psychopaths use language about conscience, illustrating how we equate conscience with the care/harm Ethical Zone.

But just telling people they should have a conscience doesn't work; the amygdala is a part of the older reptile brain. This may be another reason why teaching ethics doesn't really change anything. A workshop on teaching ethics I attended tried to activate people's care/harm Ethical Zone using journaling, music videos, and scenes from movies. That wouldn't work if the person's amygdala wasn't responsive.

Literature about psychopaths focuses on the less than 1 percent of the population who have committed egregious crimes and are in prison. Sometimes businesspeople are labeled as psychopaths because they make decisions without considering the harm that they do to others.

One study among businesspeople estimated that 4 percent of them might be psychopaths. It's obviously not an actual diagnosis but instead reflects the harm that researchers perceive that businesses can do to people when they aren't operating from the care/harm Ethical Zone.

Interestingly, two hormones affect the care/harm Ethical Zone. High levels of testosterone appear to block high levels of empathy, and high levels of oxytocin (the hormone that is released among mothers when they see pictures of their babies) promote high care/harm importance. Not surprisingly given the effect of hormones, women in general have higher levels of the care/harm Ethical Zone and are more likely to be Liberal. Again, just like the fact that care/harm is situated in the amygdala, we can't change this.

The groups of people who have the strongest emphasis on care/harm are Liberals, and importance is strongest among the youngest. This is a powerful emotion, especially among millennials who place particular importance on care/harm.

It's not that Conservatives don't care about others; they place equal importance on all the Ethical Zones, so they are less extreme than Liberals. Among Conservatives, the care/harm Ethical Zone interacts with the other Ethical Zones that are equally important to them (belonging, authority, sacredness, and fairness), while for Liberals, care/harm mostly interacts with fairness.

Thus, the reactions that Conservatives have out of the care/harm Ethical Zone look very different than those that Liberals have, even though both may be operating from the same Ethical Zone. This is why Conservatives don't respond in the same way to the stories that "bleeding-heart" Liberals find compelling.

> *It's not that Conservatives don't care about others; they place equal importance on all the Ethical Zones, so they are less extreme than Liberals.*

THE CARE/HARM ETHICAL ZONE AND ETHICS

As I REFLECT on the numerous books that I have read about ethics, it strikes me that writers say businesses need to stop focusing so much about money (the Ethical Zone of rationality and reason, as discussed in the next chapter) and care more about people (the care/harm Ethical Zone).

One manifestation of this concept is the Conscious Capitalism organization, which places at its core having a higher purpose. Another appearance of this phenomenon is a new form of corporation called benefit corporations (US) or community interest corporations (UK). Benefit corporations are companies dedicated to a "triple bottom line" of "people, planet, and profit," and they have become some of the fastest growing companies in the United States, such as Warby Parker, Etsy, and Stony-field Organic.

Some businesses have the care/harm Ethical Zone at their foundation, like healthcare. After all, what is the core of healthcare except caring for people? An example is St. Joseph's Aspirin, which has incorporated a heart into its logo and uses the line "put a little love in your heart." (Note: Although the picture of a heart in the logo does accurately connote the use of the product to prevent heart attacks, the love in the phrase takes it a step further, placing the message clearly into the care/harm Ethical Zone.)

I believe that having the care/harm Ethical Zone at the core of your business holds you to a higher standard than for other businesses.

The toy industry is another that has the care/harm Ethical Zone at its core—care for children. Children particularly need care from adults, which makes it a powerful association. Violation of this zone will cause an uproar, for example, if it is discovered that a toy hurts a child either literally (toys that children can swallow, for example) or even hypothetically (toys that collect data that can be used against the child in the future).

Care for the children must be at the core of any toy business. If not, it will run the risk of alienating its customers. (Full disclosure: I used to work for a toy company and on advertising for children's cereal before my work in pharmaceuticals.)

Many businesses popular with millennials, such as TOMS shoes— which gives away a pair of shoes for every pair you buy—have used the Ethical Zone of care/harm for its messaging, even though it isn't at the core of the business.

The origin story of TOMS illustrates how the founder came to add the care/harm zone to the business. TOMS was founded when Blake Mycoskie (no, his name isn't Tom) was traveling in Argentina and saw the effect that giving a pair of shoes had on a child. Suddenly, children's lives were changed. Two brothers who were sharing one pair of shoes that was too large and alternating going to school (because the school required shoes) could now both go to school.

Mycoskie had the thought to not just give away the shoes, but rather to sell shoes with the promise that for every shoe you buy, the company would give a pair to a needy child.

The business took off, growing 300 percent a year for the first five years and becoming a hit with millennials. Mycoskie is quite clear on what the corporate social mission does for TOMS: "It allows us to build an emotional bond with customers and motivate employees, because they know they are shopping and working for a movement bigger than themselves."

The success of TOMS has spawned a movement, now called social enterprise, which seeks adding social value to differentiate the company from its competitors. Besides TOMS and Warby Parker's eyeglasses, many companies are giving away their products such as Bombas, Everything Happy, Hand in Hand Soap, WeWood, and Headbands of Hope.

I found a list of thirty-five such companies at Influence Digest (https://influencedigest.com/business/top-35-socially-conscious-companies-that-give-back/). I am sure there are many more. During one season on *Shark Tank*, it seemed as if every third company was trying to use the "buy one, give one away" business model.

Other examples of companies using this practice are when your drugstore or grocery asks you to donate to world hunger or when it sponsors a breast cancer race or when the hotel chain offers to donate to a hunger charity if you book with them directly instead of through a third party (see the Omni Hotels Goodnight to Hunger campaign).

Cultural Aspects

Care/harm is strongest in the WEIRD areas: Western Europe, Australia, and the US and Canada. People in the developing world place higher importance on the other Ethical Zones. It's not that care/harm isn't important to them; it just interacts with the other Ethical Zones. This interaction is what leads to violations of care/harm that we Westerners can't imagine, such as women being killed for having violated the sacredness Ethical Zone when they were raped, female genital mutilation, and others.

Other ethnic groups in the West are lower in the care/harm Ethical Zone than Liberals, but that is not often recognized. The local director who embezzled in the story about the African hospital mentioned in the belonging chapter was probably lower in the care/harm Ethical Zone (for the future patients) than he was for the belonging Ethical Zone.

CONSOLIDATING WHAT WE LEARNED

THE CARE/HARM ETHICAL Zone is at the core of what most people mean when they think of ethics. It is extremely high among Liberals and moderately high among Conservatives. But it looks different among the two groups. Among Conservatives it is mediated by the other Ethical Zones (belonging, authority, sacredness, and fairness). Among Liberals, care/harm mostly interacts with fairness.

The care/harm Ethical Zone is based on reactions in the amygdala and is influenced by levels of two hormones: testosterone and oxytocin. Some products have the care/harm Ethical Zone at the core of their business, such as pharmaceuticals or toys.

The risk of being a business based in the care/harm zone is that it holds businesses to a higher standard, opening it up to criticism that doesn't occur with other businesses. Alternatively, some businesses use care/harm as borrowed interest. That borrowed interest can be closely tied to the purpose of the business (like the businesses that give away their product) or can be more loosely tied (like collecting donations for a worthy cause or using images in their advertising).

The care/harm Ethical Zone explodes our hearts, creating an opportunity for connection, but also opens us up to manipulation and has the potential to create chaos if it is violated. This risk is highest among Liberal target audiences.

6
RATIONALITY AND REASON

H UMANS ARE RATIONAL, aren't they?

Economists still use a "homo economicus" who makes rational choices in their econometric models even today, but Daniel Kahneman, Amos Tversky, and Richard Thaler (and many others) have upended that conclusion with their extensive work in cognitive psychology and behavioral economics.

In his book, *Thinking, Fast and Slow*, Kahneman talks about System 1, which makes fast decisions where we spend most of our time, and System 2, which is slow and is rarely used. System 2 is the source of rationality and reason. He mentions how we humans often give reasons for our actions, but we are really just coming up with rationalizations to justify the System 1 fast decision-making. In this world, we need to operate fast, and System 1 is how we do it. We don't have time to always be in System 2.

Moral foundations theory created by Jonathan Haidt (and collaborators), which asserts that our reactions depend on moral foundations, represents another way System 1 operates. Rationality is violated. When people act out of these nonrational Ethical Zones, it seems to others that their actions don't make sense, which is what psychologists love to study. And, in fact, this is one of the criticisms made of people who don't seem to vote in their best interest.

But sometimes people do make choices that make sense on a rational basis. This is Kahneman's System 2 or what Steven Pinker calls market pricing/rational legal. Scholars say that the ability to reason emerges when societies get large enough, when the population density of population and specialization of labor create the kind of conditions that promote development of the kind of thinking that this Ethical Zone requires. Societies that once had specialization of labor and/or dense population, but had a reduction in population, go backward in their skill level. Thus, this Ethical Zone is weaker in rural communities.

Here is the completed Ethical Framework, which adds rationality and reason:

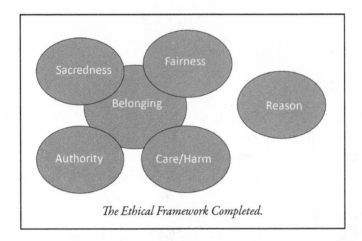

The Ethical Framework Completed.

I've put reason outside of the previously discussed zones in the diagram because it works differently. Even though reason can outvote the others, it isn't as emotionally laden as the others. Let's dig into it in more detail.

Take these examples of how, when the rationality and reason benefits of either money or convenience bump up against another Ethical Zone, rationality sometimes wins:

- A boarded-up store in rural Georgia with a sign out front "American Owned and Operated" promoted belonging and community, which wasn't enough to keep them in business.
- Just a few miles away, the parking lot at Walmart is packed, leading to the closure of small stores in rural areas (like the one just mentioned) because Walmart has lower prices despite their strong belonging and community Ethical Zone.
- On the other end of the political spectrum, a hip, urban fair-trade clothing store in Cincinnati struggles to make sales, when even as those who believe in that cause shop at stores where the clothes are cheaper but are made in sweatshops in the Far East.
- Environmentalists who march for climate change but who let

their need for convenience trump that by getting restaurant takeout in containers that contribute to excess waste in landfills or let their family's need for transportation or their physical size needs (like a 6 foot 7 frame) overcome their beliefs in climate change by buying an SUV.

An article in the *New York Times* entitled "The Tyranny of Convenience" points out the degree to which we allow convenience to dictate our choices. I would add that financial reasons are also a driver.

You could say that these people aren't acting on their beliefs, as one set of academics did in their book, *The Myth of the Ethical Consumer*. Or you could interpret these pieces of data to mean that when there is a conflict between the Ethical Zone of rationality and reason and the other Ethical Zones, the trade-offs that people make vary. Sometimes they will act on the more instinctual Ethical Zone, and sometimes they will choose the most rational choice. This is an intention-behavior gap.

REASON MAKES THE MODERN WORLD POSSIBLE

ALTHOUGH MONEY HAS been used and trade has gone on for centuries, the use of reason in everyday life is a relatively recent phenomenon. The Phoenicians were active traders before Christ was born, and the Silk Road between China and Europe was used as early as 2000 BCE, but trade did not become an integral part of everyday life until the advent of early capitalism during the Renaissance.

This Ethical Zone has become stronger as capitalism has become more and more entrenched in our society. Individualism is also part of this Ethical Zone, which has acted to counter the effects of the belonging and community and respect for authority Ethical Zones.

Modern inventions such as electricity and indoor plumbing rely on the use of reason and rationality, which has led to increased productivity and improvements in quality of life. Our lives would be shorter without the discovery of how diseases spread, how to control infections and the invention of drugs and vaccines to treat and prevent diseases.

Without this Ethical Zone, we wouldn't have an in-depth understanding of history or of psychology, both of which are crucial to our understanding exactly what happened in the past, so that we don't have to repeat it.

Some other elements of the developed world society that are possible because of this Ethical Zone are the stock market, borrowing money, and data sets. Without it, there would be no statistics and probability, and no models to try to understand and predict why people act the way they do. There would be no credit cards, or mortgages to buy a home, or student loans without the reason and rationality Ethical Zone.

The assembly line was created as part of the application of this Ethical Zone. People prefer the craftsmanship of individually created items, but we depend on machine-created parts that make cars, trains, and planes work flawlessly (usually). These inventions and other machine-produced items have increased our standard of living, but also importantly brought many types of goods within reach of the poorer citizens of the world that they could not afford when they were so expensive and were only available to the rich.

An example of the effect of this on everyday lives is provided by an analysis of the cost of artificial light. In the fourteenth century, the only source of light after the sun went down was from tallow candles, which were unsafe and totally unaffordable for the poor, so the poor had to do without and go to bed when the sun went down.

In the eighteenth and nineteenth centuries, the poor began to be able to afford artificial light using gas and kerosene, which was also safer than candles. The advent of electricity represented another major decrease in cost and increase in safety of artificial light. Over the centuries, the cost of artificial light was reduced by a factor of 11,800—an unbelievable reduction and a huge improvement in both safety and quality of life.

The system of norms of the rationality and reason Ethical Zone is worked out by reason. Formal rules don't feel normal and natural; it violates our natural inclinations of the other Ethical Zones. This is why some people have such trouble with the rules they feel are wrong to them.

This same discomfort is also behind our odd relationship with money. We need it and depend on it, but many of us feel conflicted about our desire for it because we aren't comfortable in the rationality and reason Ethical Zone. Instead, we likely spend most of our time in one of the other Ethical Zones.

What makes this an Ethical Zone instead of just a counterweight to the other Ethical Zones is how intensely we feel when it is violated. Violations of the reason and rationality Ethical Zone include stealing, thievery, and cheating. Convenience, speed, and efficiency are also part of this Ethical Zone.

Those of us in WEIRD countries switch back and forth between the reason and rationality Ethical Zone and the other zones discussed earlier depending on the situation. For example, we may trade hosting dinner parties with friends, but they would be offended if we offered them money because it violates the belonging and community Ethical Zone.

In contrast, in a restaurant we are in the reason and rationality Ethical Zone, so we pay with money and we don't offer to host them in our house to repay them. We don't think about it; we have learned this instinctively. Someone from a less developed country would probably find this switching back and forth depending on context confusing, but we do it without thinking.

The moral philosophy of utilitarianism is an expression of the rationality and reason Ethical Zone because it asks for the best for most people, which requires data. This often is in conflict with what feels right according to the care/harm Ethical Zone. The rationality and reason Ethical Zone is further developed when people go to college and when they read books such as Pinker's *Better Angels of Our Nature* and McAfee's *More from Less* and other books that use data to challenge and help us overcome our in-going perceptions. The website www.FiveThirtyEight.com that uses statistical models for journalism could only exist in a society that values rationality.

Sometimes the rational doesn't win and facts don't persuade. Our other Ethical Zones overcrowd the statistics. As mentioned earlier, people are more scared of the stuff that feels dangerous (like sharks and nuclear power) than the substances or activities that actually cause more harm (like drowning at the beach and carbon emissions). Safety experts ask us to pay attention to both the statistics and our feelings. In his book, *More from Less,* McAfee calls for us to try to overcome irrational fears about nuclear power, GMOs, and vaccines and pay attention to the data.

A different example of an Ethical Zone crowding out the rational is that knowledge about climate change doesn't change Conservatives' opinions about it. Their desire to belong overcomes their own individual reasoning. This is what psychologists call motivated reasoning—when we pick and choose facts to support what we already believe.

Motivated reasoning affects people on both sides of the aisle. An example from the Liberal side of the equation would be conservationists with data to show that deer hunting benefits the overall environment (remember, data come from the rationality and reason Ethical Zone) but don't say anything publicly because most conservation organizations are dominated by people with extremely high care/harm Ethical Zones. If they said anything positive about hunting, they are probably afraid that they would be vilified.

The rationality and reason Ethical Zone has allowed our world to develop very complex mechanisms, so involved that we don't really know how items work. We know about objects like toilets and zippers, but unless it is in our area of specialty, when asked to give details, most of us soon realize that we don't actually know that much about it. This is called the illusion of explanatory depth. Thus, most of us rate ourselves more highly on understanding these objects than is actually true. This provides a clue for one technique to have constructive conversations, which I will come back to later.

Two Kentucky women (Sarah Stewart Holland and Beth Silvers) have worked hard to overcome their belonging Ethical Zone by applying rationality and reason to issues. They came from different choirs—Sarah from the left and Beth from the right. Because they had been friends for a long time, they were determined to be polite and "grace filled."

In their book, *I Think You're Wrong (But I'm Listening)*, they highlight the process they followed of "taking off their partisan jerseys" (the belonging and community Ethical Zone) to look at the facts and how the facts surprised them. They gathered an audience for their podcast, Pantsuit Politics, who found the process enlightening and the difficulty experienced by Beth and Sarah entertaining. They found that applying the rationality and reason Ethical Zone is hard work. Most of us don't do so because it is so hard.

Applying the rationality and reason Ethical Zone is hard work. Most of us don't do so because it is so hard.

BUSINESSES RELY ON RATIONALITY TO MAKE DECISIONS

STEVEN PINKER ENDORSES the idea that societies have been evolving toward heightened rationality. I ran across the concept of the rational winning in the long run over the other Ethical Zones at the end of his lengthy tome about violence, *Better Angels of Our Nature*. In it, he pulls together Haidt's moral foundations theory with theories by two anthropologists (Alan Fiske and Richard Shweder) and creates a case for the idea that we, as a society, have been evolving where we use reason more and more.

Fiske has tied the development of rationality to the increase in population; operating in larger societies requires different skills. Specialization of labor increases the knowledge base we have. I believe that this is one reason why large companies have come to dominate our marketplace. They have people with very narrow skill sets who are just a bit better than those working at small companies, which ends up giving them an advantage.

Pinker makes the point that those of us in WEIRD countries are more able to reason than we used to be, citing how scores in the reason section of the IQ test have increased over the last century. What people may not know is that the norm of the IQ scores (IQ=100) has been changing over time to reflect the underlying population scores and has been going up steadily over the last century. The changes have been dramatic.

The 100 IQ score that someone scored in recent years would be equivalent to the test results of a genius a century ago. This change has been only in the reason section. This reflects that people didn't need reasoning skills in their work as often when they were farming as they do today to work in white-collar jobs.

Pinker takes this a step further, examining how violence and rationality are related, concluding that the increased use of reason has caused a decrease in violence because reason gives people new skills to solve problems. In his view, commerce has been a major source of the expanded use of reason.

To survive in modern society, you need skills based on reason to accomplish tasks such as calculating the price of items and deciding which is a better deal. I think he is right. When we interact with businesses, we use money and we make decisions in ways that make sense financially, and we learn to ignore our intuitive Ethical Zones because they don't work as well in that context.

But when businesspeople ignore the other Ethical Zones, they become hardened to crucial facts about our humanity, and to the fact that others are evaluating their decisions and our actions in terms of the human Ethical Zones they touch, and not just in terms of money.

To illustrate how the difference plays out in business versus broader society, consider that 82 percent of the public believes it is unethical to raise prices after a hurricane, but only 24 percent of MBA students do. In evaluating this scenario, consumers are using their instinctual fairness Ethical Zone; businesspeople are using their rationality and reason Ethical Zone. Until businesspeople learn to be aware of the Ethical Zones and how they work, they will keep running into disconnects like these.

What is behind the difference? Business decisions demand detachment. Business requires analysis. Decisions must make sense financially. A different part of the brain is used in analysis (the frontal cortex), so it's not surprising that people (even if they have empathy in other parts of their lives) don't use their amygdala to make business decisions. Even if they are going to lose money if they don't raise prices, it doesn't matter to the public at large because they aren't using their frontal cortex the way the businessperson is. They are using their amygdala, and the amygdala *can't count*. The frontal cortex takes care of counting.

In modern society, people who only use reason and don't use the care/harm zone are called psychopaths. Similarly, when businesspeople only use reason and not care/harm, they are often considered to be psychopathic. Another group who may be dominated by reason and rationality are those who are on the autism spectrum. They tend to be low in emotion and high in rationality. One commentator on the history of ethics felt that the originator of utilitarianism, John Stuart Mill, might have had autism.

An illustration of the Ethical Frames model that represents how businesspeople and those on the autism spectrum might look at issues might look like this, with reason much larger than the others.

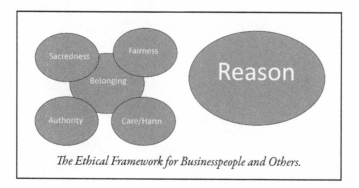

The Ethical Framework for Businesspeople and Others.

That is very different than the previous versions. In Steven Pinker's latest book, *Enlightenment Now*, he again tries to create a case that we should use rational thinking but recognizes that that isn't enough. He proposes that we increase our use of compassion, which is part of the care/harm Ethical Zone.

I think his idea has merit, but I would broaden it to include that those in business need to become aware of and sensitive to *all* the Ethical Zones. They are all real, they all have been evolutionarily useful, and they also have benefits to society today. They are also physiologically based, so we can't change them. When we don't consider these Ethical Zones, we are judging others and being condescending. Instead, we should respect them, try to understand them, and collaborate with them where they are and incorporate them into our decisions.

CONSOLIDATING WHAT WE LEARNED

RATIONALITY HAS BEEN associated with the evolution of larger societies and is the basis on which businesses have been built. Our modern world was formed by the inventions created by engineers and scientists and our understanding of history by historians using their rationality and reason Ethical Zone. All of these have contributed to vastly increased quality of life. Steven Pinker makes a case that commerce and rationality have contributed to lower levels of violence in society.

But we are in conflict when the Ethical Zone of reason pulls us in a different direction than the other Ethical Zones.

7
THE CHOIRS: CONSERVATIVES VS. LIBERALS

S O FAR, WE have learned that all humans have the same Ethical Zones, that some of them are evolutionarily based, and that our conflicts are often based on different interpretations and different importance levels of those Ethical Zones.

Here is the Ethical Framework of the six Ethical Zones that you have seen before that describes how they interact.

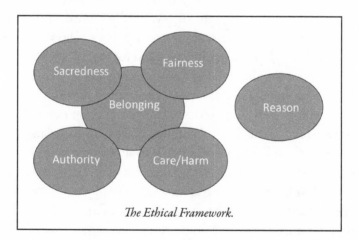

The Ethical Framework.

Now let's look in more detail at each side.

A few facts about the world of Liberals and Conservatives to keep in mind as you read this book. The percentage of the US population who consider themselves Conservative is larger than those who are Liberals. In 2017, 35 percent of adults considered themselves Conservatives versus 26 percent Liberal. The lead Conservatives have over Liberals is declining.

That isn't because the Conservative base is shrinking. Instead, Liberals are growing because moderates are becoming more Liberal.

As has been mentioned earlier, the alignment of worldview and political parties is relatively new, within just a decade or two. There used to be conservative Democrats and liberal Republicans. In that era, racism and xenophobia were the kiss of death to Pat Buchanan's campaigns for the Republican nomination in 1992 and 1996. Donald Trump has had a change of heart since he denigrated Pat Buchanan in 2000 as a Hitler lover. This recent alignment has had a large impact.

Some of this alignment may have occurred as a result of the economic events that put stresses on Conservative culture. The stresses of the September 11 attacks, the financial crisis and the resulting Great Recession, the globalization of trade and automation of manufacturing all have dealt blows to life as usual for Conservatives. This loss of security may have led to increased reliance on the belonging and community Ethical Zones than before. Further, the suspicion of Liberal culture may be the glue that holds the Conservative movement together.

As I described earlier, Liberals and Conservatives feel very differently about society. Liberals look to the future, are dissatisfied with the present, think about the world systematically, and focus on how they think it should change. Van Jones says Liberals stand for justice, which may be just another way of saying the equality flavor of fairness.

On the other hand, Conservatives come out of a worldview in which the past is valued. G. K. Chesterton observed in 1909 that conservatism is the "democracy of the dead." Frederick Hayek, an Austrian economist, suggested that the role of conservatism is to slow down undesirable developments proposed by Liberals. A more extreme example is that after the French Revolution, Conservative writer Joseph de Maistre wanted to return France to the time when the divine rule of monarchs was accepted without question, during the Middle Ages. Conservatives also value individual action and accountability over systemic action and are concerned about practicality.

Liberals and Conservatives have different views of humanity. Because of their optimistic worldview, Liberals believe humans are basically altruistic and that systems are the cause of any problems. Reflecting their gloomier worldview, Conservatives believe that people are basically bad and that systems are necessary to restrain people from their worst impulses. The paradox is that both of these viewpoints have some truth to them. Ironically, Liberals push for systemic change, but trust the systems less, which means that they trust the change less.

Geographically, Conservatives are located more often in areas with less dense populations and more in the middle of the country than on the coasts. Demographically, Conservatives are more likely to be older and more likely men with lower levels of education. There is also a difference in occupation.

Liberals are more likely to be in jobs that require a dense population (such as cab drivers) or an advanced education while Conservatives hold jobs that require more open space (such as oil workers) or are not tied to education. Even doctor specialty varies: Conservatives are more likely to be primary care doctors, while infectious disease specialists are more likely to be Liberal.

The book *Makers and Takers* by Peter Schweizer summarizes data on Conservatives versus Liberals. According to his sources, Conservatives are

- More satisfied with their lives, their professions, and their health
- More generous
- Less likely to become angry and seek revenge

However, it should be noted that the word *Conservative* has been recently recognized to be imprecise. I ran into this at my first presentation on this topic, when a "Conservative" member of the audience became upset at his results on the standard moral foundations quiz. I later came to understand that he was upset because there are two different types of Conservatives: social Conservatives and economic Conservatives. Political science research has documented this.

Social Conservatives are the larger of the two, so their data dominate. Even though this term is imprecise, I'll continue to use it because, until recently, all the data have been collected using it. If you are reading this and consider yourself a Conservative, but don't agree with the data on Conservatives, you are probably an economic Conservative.

Throughout most of the book, I have referenced that Conservatives and Liberals place different importance on the Ethical Zones. Instead of the previous graphics of the model where the Ethical Zones are all evenly sized and spaced, I would claim that the Ethical Zones among Conservatives look more like the following diagram, with belonging sized larger than the others. Note how fairness and care/harm and sacredness and authority are equally sized, reflecting their relatively equal importance. Also note how interrelated each of the original five Ethical Zones overlap with belonging. But there is no overlap with reason.

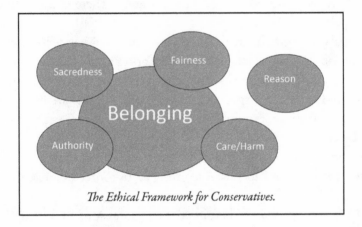

The Ethical Framework for Conservatives.

In contrast, Ethical Zones for Liberals would look much different. In the next diagram, you see that fairness and care/harm are the largest, overwhelming belonging, which is smaller but still exists. Sacredness and authority are still there, but smaller than for Conservatives.

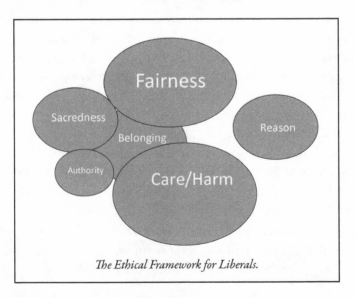

The Ethical Framework for Liberals.

According to Schweizer's data, Liberals are

- More likely to take care of themselves first and less likely to care for others
- More focused on money
- More interested in leisure than in work
- More prone to depression and nervous breakdown
- More likely to be dishonest
- Less knowledgeable about civic affairs
- More likely to be anxious

Keep in mind that these are all averages and skews. There are many individual variations that I mentioned, such as variations on how important the sacredness Ethical Zone is.

There are tender areas for both choirs, but they are different. Conservatives value all Ethical Zones approximately equally, but their hot buttons are for the ones that Liberals don't value—the belonging, authority, and sacredness Ethical Zones. Liberals react to violations of the care/harm and fairness Ethical Zones much more strongly than the others. And reason can act as a place where people can join, like Sarah Stewart Holland and Beth Silvers did in their Pantsuit Politics podcast.

When we recognize the Ethical Zones behind these choirs, we can use them in such a way that we can hear each other.

The alignment of worldview and political parties is relatively new, within just a decade or two.

8
THE RED CHOIR: DEEP DIVE INTO CONSERVATIVES

I F YOU ARE a Liberal, you have probably been reading news coverage about those who supported President Trump and thinking, how could they say those things? It's easy to dismiss them as prejudiced folks who are dying out.

Keep in mind that the news media go for the extremes, not the average or middle. It isn't news if it isn't extreme. One estimate is that the segment of devoted Conservatives represents 6 percent of the population. Another 19 percent are traditional Conservatives while 15 percent are moderates who may hold some Conservative values.

It's easy to write a caricature of Conservatives based on the media coverage of Trump supporters. What is harder is to write a sympathetic profile. This and the next chapter are my attempt to illustrate how Conservatives and Liberals would integrate the Ethical Zones into their lives. These are imaginary scenarios based on conversations I have had or sources I have read.

Conservatives value what they have right now and what they had in the past. Keeping order is important to them. Psychological tests show that they are higher in conscientiousness (on average) than Liberals but lower on openness, two of the major five personality attributes.

Let's do a reconnaissance into the life of a Conservative. Note that this is a social Conservative, not an economic Conservative. As you read this, try to figure out what you like about these people and what kind of impact they have on the people around them and their world. And listen for what makes them erupt.

> *Conservatives value what they have right now and what they had in the past.*

Rick is fifty-six years old and served in the army in the Gulf War. He lives in a small town in the Midwest and works on the assembly line in a plant that makes automotive parts. He is married with two kids. His son is in the army, stationed in Afghanistan. His daughter is a junior in high school and considering becoming a nurse. When their kids were young, his wife stayed at home with their two kids but now works as a receptionist in a legal office. In his words:

> *I was born and raised in this town and this is where I intend to die. I do what I can to help out here. My daddy and granddaddy worked real hard to make this town a terrific place to live, and I do my part. It's tough to see the people moving away and not caring what happens to their hometown.*
>
> *The Walmart moved in thirty years ago and that killed downtown. People I know lost their livelihoods when that happened, but that Walmart has more stuff and is cheaper, so you can't fight it. I shop there, and so do they, in fact, some of them work there. But those storefronts are still empty, it's real sad.*
>
> *I am on the Board of Trustees at the church downtown. The pastor is a real hell-fire-and-damnation preacher, just like we had when I was growing up. He sets a high standard for behavior. He makes sure we know what the right thing to do is. I tithe 10 percent of my income to support it.*
>
> *My old homeroom teacher, Miss Adelia, and her sister, Miss Leila, need my help to be able to stay in their home; otherwise, they would have to go into one of those nursing homes. I do what I can for her. I use my pickup truck to haul stuff for her. My whole family got involved. My wife picked out new shrubs to replace the overgrown ones at the house, and my son helped me dig them out*

when he was home on leave. My niece goes over there to sit with them and do indoor chores.

My neighbor down the street, Julie, has a son who is one of them homos. He left after high school and went to Chicago. He's the same age as my Sam and was always kind of weird growing up. Didn't want to be on the baseball team and was in the school plays. He got teased a lot then. He's grown up and is in fashion now, has done real well for himself. I am not in favor of the gay lifestyle—having sex in those gay baths sounds disgusting—but I have met his "husband" when they came back to visit Julie and he seems real nice.

Even though he is gay, Julie's son came from here, so he's one of us. I guess it's better for them to be married than having sex with lots of people, so I am okay with gay marriage. Now they are talking about adopting an orphan. Family is important.

The work I do is tough, but I am still able to do my part. I am on my feet all day, so I need high quality work boots. Every Friday, me and my buddies from the plant go out to Joe's for a couple of beers and a game or two of pool—sometimes we shoot darts.

I am concerned that the big bosses will close down the factory and move our jobs to Mexico or China or somewhere else. There's no other jobs around, so if that happens, I'm in trouble. I've heard that if they do that, they will give us money to "retrain" but for what? I don't want one of them desk jobs. I didn't like school and I don't like to sit still. The job I have suits me just fine.

I can't see moving away to get another job. I've lived here my whole life, and all my family and friends are here. My wife is working, so if that happens, we will get by. I don't think I would like to live in the city, there's no space. Some of my buddies have tried working on the oil fields because they could make a bunch of money, but they got too lonely and came back. Plus, all my friends are here. What would Miss Adelia and her sister do if I wasn't here to take care of them?

My buddy Jim got hurt on the line and started taking them

opioids and now he's addicted. Just like my buddies from the army, he's one of us, so when he can't make it to work, we guys fill in for him. The line manager knows but he doesn't tell the big shots from out of town. They wouldn't understand. They don't know what it is like to work the line and need your paycheck. I know we can't protect him forever, so I hope he shakes it off real soon before the suits find out. They might make him go to rehab.

Prejudice: I know those Liberals think people like me are prejudiced but I am really not. I have a buddy at work who is black, and I also work with a couple of immigrants. They pull their weight, so they are okay. I just am concerned about our way of life being taken over by people who aren't like us. Why don't they make their own country better rather than come here and ruin ours?

My son is in the army, just like his dad and his granddad. We have a family tradition of supporting our country. He's on his second tour of Afghanistan. I worry about what he will do when he gets out of the army, there's not much here for young people to do, especially if the factory closes down. He's married, with two kids, and another one on the way. We do a lot for our daughter-in-law and our grandkids. My daughter wants to be a nurse. That's okay, I am just worried about her going away to college and learning to not respect our family's values.

Politics: Like the guys I work with, I voted for President Trump. He's the first politician I know of who does get us. Plus, he's rich and successful, so he knows how the world works. I don't spend time reading about the "issues." If the president says what he is doing is the best, I trust him.

On Liberals: Those bleeding-heart Liberals want to ruin the country. They think it doesn't matter if we bring a bunch of immigrants into this country. We have to beat them or else they will destroy what I love about this country.

Travel: My parents went on a cruise to Bermuda last year. Now that they are retired, they are talking about going to Europe. They will go on one of the tours so that they can be sure to understand everything and won't get lost. That doesn't interest me.

Once a year, I take my family on road trips in our RV to see the western part of our beautiful country. We usually go to a national park, but we stay off-site in private campgrounds because they have clean bathrooms and showers. For my other vacation, I go fishing or hunting with my buddies.

Food: My wife works, but she gets home in time to make dinner every night, and we have dinner together as a family. She is a fantastic cook. She has a regular schedule that she follows so that I know exactly what will be on the table each night, like Monday night being meatloaf night. We go out to eat once a week, usually to the diner. I always get the same thing, but sometimes we'll go out somewhere else when my son is home.

Abuse: I hear about the sex abuse going on; the women who say they were assaulted by Harvey Weinstein shouldn't have put themselves in that position. If they didn't put themselves in that position, he wouldn't have been able to do that. I like the way Mike Pence handles it; he keeps himself from being in that position. But the stuff with Catholic priests and kids, that's sick and disgusting. It's kids, that's what makes it so bad, they are so innocent. They didn't do anything to deserve that.

Note the loyalty to the various groups that he belongs to: his former school teacher and her sister, his coworkers and his line manager, his neighbors, his army buddies. He is also loyal to his community. He served in the armed forces and now his son does. If we didn't have people like Rick and his son, the US wouldn't have as strong an armed force as it does. We need to honor him and his family (belonging and community).

Note also his willingness to follow directions if the line manager says so, his support of his hell-fire-and-damnation minister, and his trust of President Trump (respect for authority). Note that he makes decisions with little information. He has a high need for cognitive closure.

Note the earning of fairness—the ethnic coworkers, the women who got abused didn't deserve sympathy because of their bad choices, but the kids were innocent and didn't deserve it (fairness).

Note the desire for orderliness in all aspects of his life (same dinner on Mondays) and his disgust at homosexual sex and the priests violating children (sacredness).

Note the commitment he has to making his corner of the world a better place. He isn't open to moving.

Note that he has changed his mind about something (homosexual marriage), and that change is related to a different perspective. He is reflecting the success of the technique of reframing that was applied to gay rights, which I will discuss later. Also note that he is so against the Liberal agenda that he is unlikely to listen to a Liberal argument; instead he is focused on winning the argument.

In his wife's (Ellie) voice:

> Rick is pretty worked up about what Liberals are doing to this country. I'm more "live and let live." Liberals have raised some good points, but they get a little extreme. I don't like the way President Trump acts, especially the stuff that he tweets, and the separation of kids from their parents at the border breaks my heart.

> My family comes first in my life. I am grateful that Rick was able to make enough money so that I could stay home to raise my kids when they were young. I did go back to work later when they were old enough to be involved in after-school activities. My job is in town and flexible. When my kids were younger, work allowed me to come in later, so I could be homeroom mom when my daughter was in middle school. This town is a safe place to raise kids; if for some reason I couldn't be there, there are many other people who would step in and help out. My kids each have a group of friends they grew up with and are really close to and can rely on.

> I met Rick when he was in the army and moved here when he got out, so I am not from here. I grew up in a suburb of Chicago, so this is different. Sometimes I feel like I will never truly belong; most everyone has lived here their entire lives, and their parents and grandparents too. That's not quite true, I am very involved with stuff here and have made some close friends.

> The church is a big part of our lives. Rick is on the trustees, and

our social life revolves around it. I am part of the church women's group, and the couples club at church does a progressive dinner every month. The minister has some definite ideas about what is right, and I listen closely to what he says because he has studied the Bible.

I try to have dinner on the table every night when Rick comes home. He likes to eat the same thing every week, so we have meal/ day pairings like meatloaf Mondays and fish Fridays. I like to try something new once in a while, and as long as I don't do it too often, he won't complain.

I hope my kids have as successful a life as Rick and I did. My oldest is in the army, and I am really proud of him. Caitlyn wants to be a nurse and help people. I want to do everything I can to support her. I am a little concerned about where she wants to study nursing, but I grew up in the suburbs and I turned out okay, so I am not as scared the way Rick is.

Note how Ellie is more moderate than Rick, a typical gender difference. Rick has the power in this relationship, they moved to where he was from, not where she was from, and she stayed home until the kids were older (respect for authority).

Ellie is more concerned about family (both the care/harm and sacredness Ethical Zones). Despite this, she has made different choices than a more Liberal woman would about raising her family. She had children when she was younger than a Liberal woman, which is typical for a Conservative family.

Again, Ellie is as involved with organizations and connected to her community even though she moved there as an adult, and doesn't always feel like she fits in. She does pay attention to what authority figures say, but she also works around them, if they make a comment or do something she disagrees with, such as when she only tries new meals occasionally.

9
THE BLUE CHOIR: DEEP DIVE INTO LIBERALS

L IBERALS, OR PROGRESSIVES, believe in the nobility of man; they believe that problems that people have are due to the restrictions that society places on them. They take for granted the freedoms and privileges of the society they were raised in and are always looking to improve the society they live in. They have a focus on the new and the novel. They also have a sunnier view about the dangers of life and want their kids to be free to explore and be curious.

Liberals place extremely high importance (much higher than Conservatives) on two Ethical Zones: care/harm and fairness. It's not that Conservatives don't place importance on those two Ethical Zones; it's just that Liberals place an extreme importance on them.

When you read or listen to news stories from a source that appeals to Liberals, the emphasis is *always* on how people have been hurt. Fairness is important to both Liberals and Conservatives, but Liberals have a different interpretation. Unlike for Conservatives, whose fairness flavor is merit, Liberals believe either that everyone deserves the same (the equality flavor) or that some people deserve more to make up for their disadvantaged history (the need flavor).

> *Liberals place extremely high importance (much higher than Conservatives) on two Ethical Zones: care/harm and fairness.*

Again, these are imaginary composites based on people I have talked to and sources I have read, which I created in order to illustrate how the Ethical Zones integrate into people's lives.

Look at the differences between the Conservative and Liberal profile and ask yourself, who would you prefer to be your neighbor? Who does more to make the world a better place?

Darryl is a forty-nine-year-old IT manager with an insurance company who lives in a big city. He's from the Midwest but went away to college for computer science. There are no IT jobs in the town where he was born, so he has never lived there as an adult, but he visits his parents every couple of years.

He commutes an hour each way to the city, and his wife is a consultant who works out of their suburban home but travels for work. They have two kids, ages ten and eight. Their son, Jonathan, is a geek, while Hayley is into her American Girl dolls. Here are his words:

> *When Jessica quit her job to work at home as a consultant, I thought our life would get a lot easier. Well, it is mostly, except when she is traveling. The more successful she is, the more she travels, and the more stressful our lives become. We hired someone to come to our house to be there when the kids come home and take them to all their activities, but she can't work longer hours when my wife is away.*
>
> *My kids can do a sleepover at their friends' sometimes, but we have to get really creative when she is on a long trip; we have had my mother come in to stay with us a couple of times, and once we had to hire a British-style nanny to come to live with us for two weeks when my wife went to China.*
>
> *I love that my wife's income allows us to take extravagant vacations. We went to the Turks and Caicos last year for two weeks to relax but, overall, our lives are pretty crazy.*
>
> *We don't eat dinner together very often. Because the kids have so many activities, they aren't home at the same time. And I get home late from work a lot. So everyone just eats when they get hungry. We tried out one of the home-meal kits, but we don't eat together enough to make it work for us. Plus, the kids are picky*

eaters, so we let them choose their favorites. We order in pizza a lot. We shop a lot on Amazon and use it even more now that we got an Alexa.

I am under a lot of pressure at work. There's a lot of cyberattacks, and I have to stay up-to-date on the latest software and the latest threats. If we get attacked, I will probably lose my job. I want to hire an AI specialist, but we can't get a visa to hire someone from abroad. Since I can't find someone here in the US who has the skills I need, I probably can't find someone to help me. I am thinking about looking for another job before this blows up. I am considering whether I should consider jobs outside this area and then either do a long-distance commute or maybe we would have to move.

My department is almost all men, mostly Asian. I have learned to love ethnic food from hanging out with them; they know the best places in the city.

The neighborhood we live in is mostly people about our age; it's a relatively new condo development. It is diverse, with lots of Asians and a few African American families. I don't know much about our town. It's almost like I am really just here to sleep, except when I go to school functions for my kids.

On the weekends, I get together with my buddies and we play squash. I haven't been to church since the last time I went to visit my folks on a holiday. I don't have time to go to church. We do all our errands on the weekends, plus I am not quite sure if I still believe in the God I was taught about as a kid. If God is so powerful, why does God allow all those bad things to happen? Plus, those right-wing pastors give me the willies.

I am really concerned about climate change. I want a world where my kids can enjoy everything the world can offer. I've signed petitions and voted for candidates who want to do something. We bought a hybrid car that I use to go to the station, but it really doesn't fit all four of us and our stuff. We use my wife's SUV for family trips even though SUVs aren't very good for the environment.

Jessica's parents are failing, and we don't know what to do. Thank goodness her sister lives near their parents, but it's not fair that she has to do everything. Jessica tries to do what she can, but between the kids' schedules and her work and travel, it's not much. Jessica doesn't have time to volunteer for the PTO, but she does make cupcakes when asked, if she is in town.

Politics: I voted for Hillary. I don't understand how people can like President Trump, he seems like an idiot. He is racist and incites violence.

On Conservatives: I don't understand the people I grew up with. When I go back to visit my folks, I hear my old high school classmates mouthing off about how immigration is ruining this country. How do they know? They don't have many immigrants in their town, just the doctor who moved there ten years ago. They sound so prejudiced. We don't talk politics with my folks. I don't want to get into a fight.

Note that he belongs to no groups. Where he lives is like a hotel. There is nothing he is loyal to, not even the company he works for.

He makes the decisions for his own life, not his manager (low in respect for authority). Note the comfort with immigrants (his belonging is to the world, not his town or his country) yet his life is chaotic. The lack of structure in his life reflects his low importance on authority and sacredness. Note the care for others—his wife's parents, the world, the environment but low involvement.

The wife's perspective:

Darryl is from a small town in Iowa, but I grew up in the suburbs of Chicago. Darryl and I met in college; he majored in computer science and I was a business major. When it came time to look for jobs, we decided to look in a city that I knew, Chicago. It isn't that far from Iowa, so we can drive to see his parents for holidays. We both got jobs in our careers and are well paid.

We waited to have kids after we got married so I could get established in my career. Boy, did having kids complicate our lives! Don't get me wrong, I love my kids and would do almost anything for them. But juggling my demanding job, the commute, and everything the kids needed was draining. We did hire a nanny, but there still wasn't enough time in the day. So I decided to start a consulting practice, working from home. That has made my life easier, most days, and we did keep the nanny for after school.

But when I travel on business, life get hairy. Then we have to patch together a bunch of people chipping in. It's hard because we don't know that many people in the town we live in, but the kids have made friends, and I know their mothers. Luckily, my mother and my sister aren't that far away, so they can fill in too. I hate to rely on Mom, though, because she isn't doing that well.

I try to get involved in my kids' schools. I go to PTA meetings, bring cupcakes, and handled organizing a booth at the school's spring festival. But that is about all I can do and stay sane.

Food is an issue in our house. I am too busy to think about dinner, and the nanny doesn't take care of dinner. I have set up a recurring food order at Amazon using Prime, so the basics are delivered, thank God. Just like all kids, ours want typical stuff like mac and cheese, but Darryl and I are more adventurous. So we order food delivered from our local restaurants, like the sushi place a few miles away or the latest ethnic restaurant. Often, the kids have already eaten by the time our food comes, so we don't eat together. They need to eat as soon as they get home from their activities because they are starved.

Notice the more egalitarian relationship between the Liberal couple. Jessica continues to work even as she finds a way to combine that with care for her kids. Jessica waited to have kids, unlike Ellie, which is typical of a Liberal family. Both Jessica and Ellie grew up in the suburbs of Chicago, but Ellie has made choices that fit with her move to rural America with her husband, such as having kids earlier, going to church, and getting involved in the community. Jessica tries to get involved a little bit, but is exhausted from trying to juggle it all, while Ellie has more time and can handle it more easily. Ellie recognizes that her husband's beliefs are more extreme than hers, while Jessica is more in sync with her husband.

10

THE BIOLOGICAL BASIS
OF RED VS. BLUE CHOIRS

PERSONALITY ATTRIBUTES, BRAIN functioning, and hormones all play a role in creating the differences between the red and blue choirs. In this chapter, I review the scientific research that documents that our differences are not just in attitude; they have a deeper origin.

These differences start early. Neurons in children and adults react differently when they see an image of an in-group member versus an out-group member. Infants spend more time looking at faces that are similar to their caregivers. In adulthood, the involuntary responses relating to the Ethical Zone of belonging and community affect saliva and sweat production.

Conservatives spend more time looking at negative images than Liberals, reflecting their gloomier worldview. Winning generates dopamine, which is the pleasure hormone. Those who are high in respect for authority tend to be higher in conscientiousness, one of the big five of the attributes that psychologists use to describe the fundamental aspects of our personality.

Conservatives are also lower on another of the big five personality attributes, openness, which is why they don't like change.

Recently, researchers have found that following commands reduces anxiety compared with making your own decisions. The respect for authority Ethical Zone means that Conservatives can relax more, while Liberals are more anxious.

Conservatives also have higher need for cognitive closure. Liberals have increased responses to the ACC (anterior cingulate cortex), which is involved in error detection and resolving conflict. This may be the cause of Liberals' greater tolerance of ambiguity, lower need for cognitive closure, and lower respect for authority.

Conservatives are also more sensitive to disgusting images, which is related to the sacredness Ethical Zone. Taking a dose of ginger (which has an antinausea effect) has been shown to tamp down disgust reactions, even on non-food-related issues, including racial resentment.

The care/harm Ethical Zone is related to production of two hormones, testosterone and oxytocin, which affect the functioning of the empathy center, the amygdala. Testosterone blocks the amygdala functioning while oxytocin promotes it, which influences the gender skew of politics.

The rationality and reason Ethical Zones rely on the frontal cortex, which can compute percentages and make cost comparisons. This is what Daniel Kahneman calls System 2 in his Nobel Prize–winning work. But System 2 uses a lot of energy and is slow, so humans don't use System 2 very often.

As I mentioned in the rationality chapter, businesspeople and those on the autism spectrum are probably higher in this Ethical Zone. And psychopaths have been shown to not use the amygdala, instead relying on rationality by using their frontal cortex.

Conflicts are related to the fact that people are using different parts of their brains when they place different importance on the different zones. For example, when Liberals are thinking pro-choice thoughts about abortion, they are probably using the amygdala, the seat of empathy and the care/harm Ethical Zone. In contrast, Conservatives may be focused on the sacredness Ethical Zone when thinking about abortion and using their anterior insula. No wonder we talk past each other!

We are all subject to motivated reasoning. Conservatives and Liberals actually perceive data differently, in such a way that supports their current perceptions.

It's not surprising that we can't convince anyone of our point of view when they are using a different part of their brain and when we are asking them to do things that go against their natural tendency.

The different Ethical Zones that I have been talking about use different parts of our brains and relate to different physiological processes and personality characteristics. That's why we can't talk to each other until we understand our differences.

It's not surprising that we can't convince anyone of our point of view when they are using a different part of their brain and when we are asking them to do things that go against their natural tendency.

But there is hope. If we can reach the Ethical Zone of understanding, we can work with people where they are. Let's go there next.

11
THE ETHICAL ZONE OF UNDERSTANDING IS THE GOAL

U P UNTIL NOW, I have been mostly drawing on moral foundations theory by Haidt and Graham and Fiske's relational models theory. Another theory that has relevance is Clare Graves's spiral dynamics theory. Although some might reject it as being too woo-woo, it is based on data he collected in the 1950s and 1960s and is consistent with much of the two other theories. Graves said that the two determinants of how a person operates are dependent on neurological equipment (we have seen that biology has an impact) and the society a person operates in (and we have seen that the environment a person grow up in has an impact).

The spiral dynamics model is difficult to understand, and I don't think it adds a lot of insight in general. But it does have a rationality stage (like the model Pinker described) and is useful because it points a potential way to the future—one that I want you to achieve by reading this book—the Ethical Zone of understanding.

To me, the most important area that Graves has included is a movement that is evolving toward a new state of being, which he called the turquoise meme or holistic self. I call it the Ethical Zone of understanding. There, a person seeks peace by developing more openness to a variety of perspectives without preferring any of them. That is what I hope you can commit to working toward. That will bring peace.

> *A potential way to the future—one that I want you to achieve by reading this book—is the Ethical Zone of understanding.*

Another key point made by the spiral dynamics theory is that we may be tempted to feel fear or disdain about the other groups. Overcoming that is part of achieving the Ethical Zone of understanding. Here's the completed Ethical Framework, where I overlay a seventh zone on top of the others:

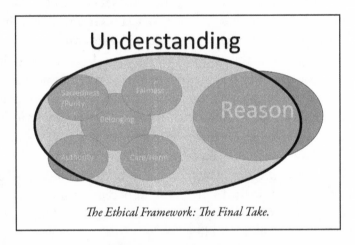

The Ethical Framework: The Final Take.

I wish I had had this framework a few years ago, when I had a difficult conversation with my elderly aunt. She was a consistent loving figure of my childhood. She was always there. While I was visiting her, she went into a tirade about immigrants in front of her full-time live-in caregiver, who was an immigrant from Poland. I thought this was very rude, and I left in a huff. I never saw her again before she died. If I had reached the Ethical Zone of understanding, I would hope I could have been more loving, once I had understood where she was coming from

Marie Curie captured the benefits of understanding when she said: "Nothing in life is to be feared, it is only to be understood. Now is the time to understand more, that we may fear less."

By reading this book, you have taken the first step toward the Ethical Zone of understanding. In the next part of this book, I will take you through how to use the Ethical Zone concepts to understand what is driving the conflicts of today. After that, I will take you through how to put that into practice.

PART II

T HIS SECTION REVIEWS the issues that are a major source of conflict in society today and analyze them by the Ethical Zones Framework. This focus on the issues will help you start to see the issues separately from the people and the values they believe in.

I don't expect you to change your mind, but I do expect you to understand the world in a new way.

in Part III, we will dig into possible ways that you can use this understanding to talk to people in a new way. Step-by-step we are building your knowledge base so you can become like the sun in the Aesop fable, where the traveler relaxes and takes off their cloak, so they can hear you in a different way as you persuade.

12
USING THE ETHICAL ZONE FRAMEWORK TO ACHIEVE UNDERSTANDING

A S WE HAVE been talking about, our society is polarized and divided and frozen. It looks like this is playing out in issues, but what is really going on is a division of values or the differing Ethical Zone Framework that different people have. Using this theory to analyze what is behind the issues of the day that don't seem to get solved, and that remain problems behind the divisions of our culture, can help us figure out ways to deal with each of the topics (which I will deal with in a later chapter).

The issues I have picked are mostly from the Liberal agenda; after all, Liberals are the ones pushing for change. And the resistance comes mostly from Conservatives. That's the point.

First, it is useful to identify the primary Ethical Zone behind each issue, but it turns out the most problematic and long-standing ones actually have multiple zones behind the issue, which makes the divisions even wider and more stubborn.

Multiple Ethical Zones = Stronger Attachments!

And then, of course, the people who are disagreeing are coming from the perspective of a different Ethical Zone, which doesn't help. Here's my analysis of the major issues of the day, using the Ethical Zones behind them to explain our differences. As you read this, don't get mad at me, I am just trying to explain what is going on, not justify. I want to help people solve these issues, not perpetuate them.

> *Multiple Ethical Zones = Stronger Attachments!*

GUN CONTROL

I RECENTLY SAW a presentation about an ad campaign that attempted to convince gun owners to lock up their guns around kids because guns are so dangerous. But the presenter had done research among gun owners that explained why the campaign was ineffective. Her research found that the gun owners didn't buy the argument that unlocked guns are dangerous to have around kids because they have taught their kids to not touch the guns.

Obviously, there are data (that is, rationality and reason) that prove that guns have killed when kids touched guns they weren't supposed to. So, there's a disconnect. The campaign creators think unlocked guns are dangerous, but the gun owners don't feel that way. That's a second disconnect. Why do they have such different perspectives?

Let's analyze the disconnects through the lens of the Ethical Zones Framework.

I've already mentioned how Brené Brown has described guns as part of the Southern Conservative culture that she grew up in. That represents the belonging and community Ethical Zone. But that isn't enough to fully explain these disconnects. I think that guns may also represent a rite of manhood, another strong part of the belonging and community Ethical Zone.

Let's also look at the parenting style favored by Conservatives, who are more likely to be gun owners. As I talked about in the chapter on respect for authority, Conservatives see the world as a more dangerous place than Liberals do. To help their kids cope with the dangerous world, they teach their kids obedience, respect for elders, good manners, and being well behaved. They believe in those values, so they trust that if they train the kids to not touch the guns, the kids will obey them. Thus, they truly expect that their kids will obey and won't touch the guns, exactly as the presenter said.

Therefore, gun owners don't buy into the entire premise of kids not doing what they are told and disobeying them—the premise that was underneath the lock-up-your-guns campaign.

Is there another part to it? I think there might be. I think gun owners might view guns as making their world safer and not more dangerous. After all, their answer to shooters in schools is to allow teachers to carry guns, and their answer to the danger of burglars is to arm homeowners.

After the shooting in the Texas church in 2019, President Trump channeled this idea in a tweet about the heroes of the day: "Lives were saved by these heroes and Texas laws allowing them to carry arms!"

This is going to be hard for Liberals to hear, but for Conservative gun owners, guns feel safe. Conservatives have many more positive experiences with guns than negative experiences. They use guns when they hunt, so guns are practical tools. Kids are routinely taught how to shoot at an early age. Because Conservatives are more likely to live in a rural area, where they don't have a police force around the corner to call on, they need a way to defend themselves. That makes guns important to a rural way of life. Guns may have become a positive part of the sacredness Ethical Zone, while they are a violation of that zone for Liberals.

In contrast to Conservatives, Liberals' experiences with guns are all negative. For Liberals, the most active Ethical Zone when talking about guns is the care/harm Ethical Zone that guns hurt people. That seems the most obvious, so that is what they use. But that doesn't work because for Conservatives, their care/harm Ethical Zone interacts with the other zones, which are positive for guns.

Thus, Liberals and Conservatives are coming at guns from exactly opposite perspectives on the sacredness/purity Ethical Zone. And the arguments by Liberals backfire when they try to convince Conservatives that guns are dangerous, because Conservatives don't believe it.

Given the polar opposite positions, it's not surprising that the split between Republicans and Democrats on gun policy is the largest of any issue measured by Pew—a fifty-seven-point gap.

IMMIGRATION AND RACE

AS WAS REFERENCED earlier, one of the core Ethical Zones for Conservatives is the belonging and community Ethical Zone. Conservatives react differently to people in their group versus people who aren't. Race and country of origin are markers of belonging or otherness. These are often lumped together by Liberals using the phrase "persons of color."

Thus, under the stressful aftermath of the September 11 attacks, increased immigration from Africa to Europe and loss of jobs due to the financial crisis, globalization, and automation, it is no surprise that the resurgence of nationalism is occurring in the developed world, especially among Conservatives. When people are doing well, they can afford to feel more open and welcoming; when they aren't, they close down. (Think Maslow's hierarchy of needs.)

The data on immigrants aren't well known. A survey of 24,000 native-born people from six developed countries showed that most of them (including those in the US) overestimated the number of immigrants in their own country. Further, these native-born people thought immigrants were more Muslim and less Christian than they are and more unskilled than they actually are. Conservatives were even more likely to believe inaccurate data. But the survey also showed that people aren't interested in hearing the accurate data. So a rationality-based argument won't work.

Nationalism and xenophobia aren't new but had been lessening as the world tilted more Liberal and open while feelings of security had been increasing. Britain joined the European Union while the world was in this relatively peaceful state after WWII. The nationalism exhibited by Brexit is a desire to return to what had been true in the past.

In the US, President Trump tapped into this nationalism with his campaign rally chant of "build the wall," the ban on immigration from non-white countries, and separation of children from parents when they were caught illegally crossing the southern US border.

The US picture is complicated by its history of slavery. Slavery was justified by otherness, and the color of skin acts as a marker that a person's ancestor was an enslaved person. Before the American Civil War, churches in the South sanctioned slavery because it was mentioned in the Bible. Thus, even though descendants of enslaved people are clearly citizens of the US, they are still considered to be others.

As I have mentioned, issues have an even stronger hold when more than one Ethical Zone is involved. Besides the belonging and community Ethical Zone, the sacredness/purity Ethical Zone is involved with the racial and immigration issue.

You can see this in the language that is used, with words like *dogs* used to describe people and when enslaved persons were counted as less than one person. This language is dehumanizing and degrading. This Ethical Zone leads Conservatives to feel less safe around immigrants and black people. While the common wisdom among Liberals is that exposure to immigrants and other people of color will eventually desensitize Conservatives with racist impulses, in fact, given this fear, it will actually just make their reactions more intense.

There is another element tied to the respect for authority Ethical Zone, and it is that of illegality and orderliness. Conservatives crave orderliness. Conservatives believe that people who break the law deserve to be punished—an intersection of the merit-based flavor of fairness and the orderliness of the respect for authority Ethical Zones.

Further, the fact that white men have had power and a white man is now president using this language means that the respect for authority Ethical Zone is involved in another way. The combination of these Ethical Zone violations makes this issue very strongly bound and difficult to counteract.

On the other side of the picture, Liberals are concerned about the well-being of all people, drawing on the care/harm Ethical Zone. The Liberal media documented the suffering by the parents and children who were separated and the poor conditions where the immigrant children were being held. It is heart-wrenching to read those stories, which is the point. But their concern is often at a distance or theoretical.

The equality flavor of the fairness Ethical Zone is also raised by Liberals, that all people are valuable and that identifying people by where they are born is really just an accident of birth. Liberals are clearly lower in the belonging and community Ethical Zone, as a text sent by one of my friends illustrates: "Merry Christmas to everyone, no matter where they are."

As measured by Pew, racial attitudes have the second highest gap between Republicans and Democrats (a fifty-five-point difference), just after gun policy. Immigration attitudes have a less extreme gap (forty-three-point difference.)

HEALTHCARE

HEALTHCARE FOR ALL has become a campaign promise in 2020 by progressive politicians, drawing on the two Liberal Ethical Zones, care/harm and fairness. Because health relates to the very essence of life, it is not surprising that healthcare has become a rallying cry for Liberals because of their extremely strong attachment to the care/harm Ethical Zone.

And the fact that not everyone has access to affordable healthcare taps into the fairness Ethical Zone because Liberals favor the equality flavor of fairness. One healthcare advocate's position can be summarized as that we are killing people if we don't pass a universal healthcare bill.

But why is there opposition to this on the Conservative side? Don't they need affordable healthcare also? Aren't Conservatives dying because they don't have healthcare?

I have been pondering this question, and I think that the opposition may not be tied into the Ethical Zones, which are the focus of this book. Instead, I believe the opposition may be related to concern about change and costs, as well as personal responsibility, choice, and not trusting the government.

Although healthcare can evoke the sacredness/purity Ethical Zone, as evidenced by the death panels comment made during the passage of the Affordable Care Act under President Obama, that comment has faded and doesn't seem to have lingered. The belonging and community Ethical Zone may also be involved because if you get healthcare insurance through your job, then that might be part of that belonging. But, also, that doesn't seem strong.

Because healthcare is not as tightly tied to any Ethical Zones, I think the divide on healthcare could be successfully bridged more easily than some of these issues, as I will talk about in a later section. In a way, this has already happened as the tie of President Obama to the Affordable Care Act has faded.

The Pew study did not have healthcare specifically broken out, but Democrats are more positive about the role of government than Republicans—a by a thirty-five point difference, just below the average.

CLIMATE CHANGE AND GLOBAL WARMING

ENVIRONMENTALISM HAS BEEN a hot issue for the past few decades, but its message has evolved.

Some pivotal moments in environmental history were Rachel Carson's 1962 publication of *Silent Spring* over the dangers of DDT, the formation of Greenpeace in 1969, and the first Earth Day in 1970, which focused on pollution. Although Earth Day was a hippie-inspired activity (read Liberal), there was an appeal to Conservatives in the corporate campaign about littering that began in 1953 with the slogan "Keep America Beautiful" (note the patriotism of belonging used in this phrase and the focus on pollution and beauty, which references the sacredness/purity Ethical Zone).

The 1971 "Keep America Beautiful" campaign became known as the crying Indian ad. It has been widely credited with inspiring today's environmental movement. Because the campaign supposedly depicted a Native American (which he was not), it probably tapped into Liberal sensibilities more than Conservative because Conservatives would have seen the Native American as an other, outside their belonging and community group.

The switch to a message of climate change began in the 1990s and gained momentum in the 2000s with the 2006 film *An Inconvenient Truth*, which documented the efforts of Al Gore to raise awareness of climate change and 2009 launch of Bill McKibben's 350.org and other similar organizations. A climate march occurred in 2014, with a follow-up march in 2017. This shifted the message from concern about litter, pollution, and beauty to concern about the future existence of the planet and of humanity.

Note that this change represents a shift in the Ethical Zones from a balance of both Liberal- and Conservative-related Ethical Zones to ones that are Liberal only. No longer is there any reference to the belonging and community Ethical Zones or the sacredness and purity Ethical Zones. The emphasis is now on the care/harm Ethical Zone. This turn has resulted in mobilizing Liberals, who are high in care/harm, but has alienated Conservatives.

Further, there is also concern that the areas disproportionately affected are populated by the poor, playing on the equality flavor of fairness, a Liberal favorite. Environmentalism in the shape of climate change is clearly in the Liberal camp now, when earlier it was not.

Climate and environmental concerns have a forty-eight-point gap (above average) between Republicans and Democrats in the Pew study.

ABORTION

BILL CLINTON INTRODUCED the topic of abortion in national politics in 1992 with the phrase that abortion should be "safe, legal and rare." This was meant to appeal to people who felt morally conflicted about abortion, which is most of us. But recently, the word *rare* has been dropped by some Liberals in order to not make those who do have abortions feel bad about their choice.

I understand why Roman Catholics are vehemently antiabortion because that is what their church and the Pope teach. They are operating under the respect for authority Ethical Zone. To paraphrase a Roman Catholic friend of mine, she has always found it easier to do what the Pope says.

But I've been a little puzzled about why Evangelical Christians have picked up the Roman Catholic teaching so passionately. They may say it's biblical, but it is not. I do realize that Evangelical Church leaders have picked up on the antiabortion theme, so the respect for authority Ethical Zone is somewhat relevant here. However, I believe that another Ethical Zone propels this issue.

What helped me step outside of my Liberal blinders was to understand that the key Ethical Zone for the antiabortion movement is the sacredness of life. For those who are Conservative, this is extremely important. Pregnant women and babies before they are born tap into the power of this Ethical Zone. This far outweighs concern for the mother's career or other life choices, which would be related to the care/harm Ethical Zone.

Sometimes, antiabortion advocates suggest that the sanctity of the baby's life should outweigh the mother's health, especially mental health. Advocates are so convinced of this, they have started a campaign to stop women from aborting children with birth defects, because all children are sacred.

And, of course, the belonging and community Ethical Zone is involved because people who are antiabortion also belong to groups that are antiabortion. So, all three Ethical Zones that are stronger in Conservatives are involved, making this issue a powerful expression of Conservative values.

Not surprisingly, Liberals are focused on care/harm for the mother, for the child after he or she is born, and sometimes for the other children in the family. On the other side, while Conservatives do care about children, in their case, care/harm is moderated by the other Ethical Zones. Thus, they feel more strongly about unborn children (because of the sacredness/purity Ethical Zone) than they do about children when they are already born and definitely more strongly than they do about the mother's image of her life and the way she wants it to be. But this is a continuum, and most people are somewhere in the middle, morally conflicted.

Keep in mind that Conservatives are more likely to provide practical help than Liberals. A Conservative friend of mine volunteers at a pregnancy center that doesn't just try to convince pregnant couples to have their baby, they also provide parenting classes and items that are needed for infants, such as car seats and cribs. Liberals are at a distance; once the abortion is over, their job is done.

The Pew study did not cover attitudes toward abortion, but another source (Gallup) shows the gap between Liberals and Conservatives over abortion are very large, with a forty-seven-point gap. (Note: The Gallup and Pew studies were not conducted in the same manner and are not directly comparable.)

HOMOSEXUALITY AND QUEERNESS

HOMOSEXUALITY AND QUEERNESS are causing conflict in our world. When I use the word *queerness*, I am including gender fluidity, nonbinary gender, transsexuality, intersex, and any other challenges to stereotypes.

This isn't an issue just in the developed world; it is causing conflict between the developed world and the developing world. The Episcopalian denomination split in 2008 over acceptance of gays and lesbians in the leadership of the church, with some churches aligning themselves with a homophobic Episcopal denomination based in Africa. I know of one mission organization that supports a hospital in a homophobic country that requires gay employees based in Africa to be celibate to avoid provoking conflict. Because of this ban, some Liberal congregations who had been supporting the hospital will no longer donate to the organization.

A more personal perspective is provided by the experience of one of my fellow students at seminary who had been a pastor in Africa. While at seminary in the US, he was exploring his sexuality and was outed on line. When his family and former congregation in Africa discovered that he was gay, they sent death threats. His African possessions were destroyed, and he was disowned by his children. Note: He is safe, he received asylum in the US. But he can never go back to his homeland and will never see his children again.

As you might expect, those who are Conservative are against the LGBTQI movement, and those who are Liberal aren't. Some of this can be explained in a simplistic way of describing the Ethical Zones of belonging and community and respect for authority. When the group you belong to and the leaders you follow say something is unethical, then you tend to follow along with what they say, if you are Conservative. Several churches have split over this issue here in the US, even among my denomination, the Quakers. But I think there is more to it than this simplistic explanation.

Homosexuality is not a modern phenomenon; it existed in biblical times, and the verses in the Bible that appear to condemn homosexuality are used by Evangelical Christians to provide proof of the evils of homosexuality. This is part of their claim to take what the Bible says literally. But that doesn't fully explain what is going on.

Actually, they don't follow everything literally as Rachel Held Evans, a popular Evangelical author and blogger who recently died, demonstrated in her book where she documented herself carrying out all the biblical instructions for women for a year.

As my Old Testament professor once said, because the Bible is a collection of books written over the course of centuries by many different people, it can be used to support any position. So, saying they are Bible fundamentalists isn't enough to help us understand the Conservative opposition to homosexuality.

What seems to really be behind the hostility against homosexuality are violations of the three Ethical Zones that are stronger in Conservatives. Beyond the simplistic explanation that their community is against homosexuality, belonging and community also involves becoming part of the tribe of your gender. Most children learn very early what gender they belong to and choose toys that their culture considers gender appropriate.

Until recently, parents of children with indeterminate genitalia were advised by doctors to use surgical methods to "correct" the child's genitalia so that the child could grow up with a clearer gender assignment. They did this because those who don't clearly belong to a gender challenge the very definition of this early lesson of the tribe they belong to. It shakes their sense of identity to the core.

This explains why ads that challenge the definition of masculinity such as Gillette's #ToxicMasculinity video and Bonobo's #EvolvetheDefinition campaign provoke extreme reactions from Conservative men. Homosexuality and queerness in general elicit strong reactions for the same reason.

More than just the simple idea that authority figures teach that homosexuality is wrong, the respect for authority Ethical Zone is involved in another way because it seems like the natural order of the world is being disturbed. Because Conservatives have a high need for cognitive closure, they don't want to hear long explanations of how homosexuality or intersex genitalia are actually natural. They expect a simpler, less complicated world.

But probably the most powerful part of the reaction against homosexuality and queerness comes out of the sacredness/purity Ethical Zone. Remember, sex is an integral part of this zone, and sex in the wrong context is "dirty." Conservatives preach to keep their body pure until marriage. A sexual relationship between two unmarried people of the same gender and other manifestations of queerness are a major violation of this Ethical Zone.

Remember that Conservatives have higher than average nausea reactions, which can be countered by administration of ginger. Homophobia is rooted in a physical reaction; it is not just a belief.

In contrast, Liberals are concerned with care for and harm against everyone, including those who do not conform to stereotypes because of their concern for the equality flavor of fairness.

Surprisingly, despite how strong these attitudes seem to be aligned with the Ethical Zones, which should predict a big gap, attitudes toward gender and sexuality only have a thirty-five-point gap, just below average. This has been improving over the past few decades, which I will discuss in a later chapter.

THE ANTIVACCINE MOVEMENT

THE CURRENT ANTIVACCINE movement represents another opportunity to examine how the Ethical Zones Framework explains attitudes and behavior that may seem incomprehensible to those not in it.

I have been paying attention to the antivaccine movement for a long time. I was commissioned to do a study of parents of children about attitudes toward vaccines in 2000, just as the movement was getting started, and I have worked in the pharmaceutical industry since then, so I have some close-up insights.

Unlike many of these issues, this movement is a surprising combination of Ethical Zones, one that doesn't follow the standard pattern. That doesn't make it any less important; it just means that averages don't tell the entire story.

Many of the people who are antivaxxers are Liberal and high in care/harm. You can identify the Ethical Zone by listening to the way they talk about how their children won't be able to handle the high load of vaccines or that they fear their children will get autism. Because the diseases their children are being vaccinated against haven't been widespread in the parents' lifetime, the risk of the diseases seems much less to them than the risk of the vaccines.

A 2018 study used moral foundations theory to ascertain that the antivaxxers were higher in the sacredness Ethical Zone than those who were not antivaccine. The results make sense. It isn't just the discredited claim that vaccines cause autism, there is more to this. Vaccines are putting what seems like a foreign substance into a vulnerable child's body, which could cause harm. In fact, some of them call drugs "poison," another tip-off that they are high in sacredness.

So even though Liberals tend to be low on the sacredness Ethical Zone generally, those who are antivaccine are more likely to be those who are high in sacredness (in the form of purity).

In 2000, before I had heard about moral foundations theory, I did a study about attitudes of parents toward children's vaccines for the Merck vaccine division. One of the main drivers of attitudes toward vaccines were attitudes toward doctors. Those who were less likely to vaccinate their kids were low on trusting their doctor. Thus, those who were antivaccine were likely to be low in respect for authority, which is similar to most Liberals. In this way antivaxxers are typical Liberals.

Therefore, a doctor-related strategy won't work for the truly anti-vaxxers. They don't trust their child's doctor, nor do they probably trust the government. They definitely don't trust the vaccine manufacturers. The government may be able to force them to comply, but it will be against their will. Care/harm is already involved, but it is care for their child. They truly believe they are doing the best for their child.

13
PRESIDENT TRUMP AND
THE ETHICAL ZONES

PRESIDENT DONALD J. Trump is an extremely polarizing figure in American politics. His approval ratings are at historically low numbers (ranging from a onetime high of 45 percent after Inauguration Day to a low of 35 percent in December 2017), and he was elected by the Electoral College despite not winning the popular vote.

His base is concentrated in certain states, and even in most of those he didn't win by a landslide. He is an instinctive politician whose positions are not typical Conservative positions, but he has been able to inspire intense loyalty among his base. How does he do it? I contend he is successful at it because his instincts are exactly on target with the three Ethical Zones that social Conservatives are higher on.

Let's look in detail at how his positions compare to the social Conservative Ethical Framework.

Note: I am leaving the economic Conservatives aside, because there isn't as much data on them. But they might be the ones who are actually responsive to President Bill Clinton's message of "It's the Economy, Stupid."

The key slogan for President Trump is "Make America Great Again." Clearly, this is a belonging and community related slogan. Note that this slogan also expresses nostalgia, a longing to return to the past. This is consistent with Conservatives' desire to preserve what is valuable about the past. One of the chants repeated at his rallies ("build the wall") is clearly also belonging related. Remember, Conservatives are higher on belonging than Liberals. Liberals' allegiance is to the world; Conservatives' community is a place, especially a country.

The other major chant ("lock her up," about his 2016 opponent Hillary Clinton) expresses the antipathy that Conservatives feel about

Liberals. Conservatives feel that Liberals are responsible for what is wrong with this country and are enjoying the suffering of the Liberals at the way that President Trump won the election. This is the common enemy form of belonging.

The Executive Orders about immigration, the Muslim ban, the separation of children from their parents at the border, and the attempt to revoke DACA are also clearly related to the belonging and community Ethical Zone.

But there is more to President Trump's instinctual play on Conservative Ethical Zones than just belonging. He evokes the implicit hierarchy of the sacredness/purity Ethical Zone in his dehumanizing word choices to describe immigrants.

As Chris Wallace mentioned on Fox News, when Trump uses the word *infestation*, it sounds like he is talking about vermin. Trump used this word when he talked about gang members in the US, when he tweeted about illegal immigrants, and when he tweeted about members of Congress who should go "back to their country."

Similarly, he also compares people to dogs as a way of denigrating them and making them lower on the implicit sacredness scale. And Conservatives are higher on sacredness than Liberals and are more likely to react to these words because they have a higher likelihood of feeling disgust. It's not even psychological; they have a physical reaction.

Trump's choice of Conservative judges who will be more likely to support pro-life positions is another major driver of his support among his followers, because it plays in this powerful sacredness Ethical Zone. This may have been the deciding factor for some people, given the importance of the abortion issue to them.

Because President Trump is a rich white man who is tall, he stimulates greater respect for authority among Conservatives than Hillary Clinton or Barack Obama could. Of course, as a black man, Obama didn't exude the normal authoritative power of a president to Conservatives.

Hillary was hobbled by the fact that she was shorter than Trump (which was obvious in the debates when he lurked behind her) and also a woman (who does not induce strong feelings of respect for authority among Conservatives).

One commentator noted that all but three presidential races in the history of the US have been won by the taller candidate. Tall equals authority. Plus, because he was successful in business and is rich, Trump fits the stereotype of an authority figure. Thus, respect for authority is another key driver of the fervor demonstrated by his supporters.

Being successful in business also may play on the merit-based flavor of fairness that Conservatives favor. In effect, some Conservatives may feel that President Trump may deserve the presidency because he earned it through his business practices and knowledge of how the world works.

President Trump had an in-going advantage of wealth, gender, height, and race in the 2016 presidential campaign that won him supporters just for those reasons. Then, he also chose issues and used language in a way that spoke directly to Conservatives, playing on their Ethical Zones, their concerns, and their fears. He also may be taking advantage of a belief that successful people deserve additional success. That became a winning combination.

President Trump also channels authority in how he demands unquestioning adherence to his way. If you work for him and don't agree with him, you will probably be fired. Representatives and Senators have to toe the line, or they are targeted by him and fear that the Trump supporters won't vote for them when they are up for reelection. Supporters feel they must be behind him all the time. There is a high degree of risk associated with being a Trump supporter. You can't question him or what he says.

> *President Trump had an in-going advantage of wealth, gender, height, and race in the 2016 presidential campaign that won him supporters.*

PART III

Now that you are able to see the issues, the values and the people as separate parts of the system, you are ready to act. Let's go!

14
PREPARATION

A S I HAVE been working on this section of the book, I struggled with what comes first in the process. These steps aren't set in stone, they can be done in any order, and you can jump around, but I believe that unless we prepare ourselves, we will fail. All of these steps could be a book in themselves, so this is just intended to be an outline of the work that is necessary and important to do to be able to bridge the gap between the two sides.

To help, I have prepared a workbook (available separately) with questions to help you along the way. Feel free to use any resources that you think will help. I also recommend doing this work in the context of a group (see the later chapter on what makes a good group) and practicing this behavior in a workshop environment. I offer workshops as a way to jump-start the process.

One observation that has been made as I talk to people about this endeavor is how much effort it takes. That's true. I have based my recommendations on work that I have done over the past few years, including my time at seminary. But, if it was easy, then we would have done it already, wouldn't we? And peace is never easy.

Another question that has come up is "What about the other side? Are they going to change?" The answer: We can't make them change. But what will change is the relationship. If a relationship is represented by A + B = C, where A is you, B is the other person, and C is the relationship, if A (you) changes, in order to balance the equation, something else has to change, either the relationship or the other person. Sometimes it is both. But I promise you, if you change, others around you will change.

As Ralph Waldo Emerson said, "Nothing can bring you peace but yourself."

> *If you change, others around you will change.*

STEP 1: LEARN ABOUT YOUR BIAS

FIRST, YOU NEED to learn about yourself and your own biases. As we know, people sometimes have misconceptions about themselves. One of those is that we tend to believe that we are objective. That's a myth. No one is objective, and no one has the entire truth. It's easy to point fingers at someone else's bias and not so easy to identify our own. Our biases are like air to us, they surround us, but we don't think about them. But we all have favorites. We are all human with human foibles and weaknesses.

In seminary, we had an assignment in which we had to identify our bias and explain how it affected our interpretation of a biblical passage. It was enlightening to see how people had dramatically altered interpretations of the same passage because of different life experiences. The interpretations were affected by people and events such as an abusive parent, a sister who made the difficult decision to transition to a man whose parents refused to accept the transition, and the type of work that people had done.

One of the elements from my past that has affected my own perspective was growing up with a mother who rejected my sister who had Down's Syndrome. Her bias affected my other sister and me differently. My sister has made working with adults with disabilities her life's work, while I chose a very different path. But when the time came to deal with end-of-life issues for my sister, I was the one to step up. We each had different responses to the same situation, which affected our worldview. This influenced my views of motherhood, the role of women, and the sacredness of life, which has made the topic of abortion very difficult for me to write about as well.

As Part I covered, your worldview is affected by your parents' worldview, their parenting style, events, your biology, and the economic conditions in which you were raised. But your adult life experience also has an impact. For me, working in major corporations also had a major impact on my worldview.

One way to get to know your biases is to take tests. The best tests produce results that not only make sense to us but also give us more insight into ourselves. The moral foundations quiz (found at https://yourmorals.org) is one way to learn about yourself.

I heard from one person who, when he took the test, was appalled that he was high on the Liberal Ethical Zones of care/harm and fairness because he considered himself Conservative. But he was probably an economic Conservative and a social Liberal. This test will help you sort out what you really believe.

Other ways are to pay attention to your thoughts when you read an article or hear an opinion you disagree with and question why you came to that conclusion. That's probably a manifestation of your bias.

STEP 2: DETACH FROM YOUR BIAS

DO YOU EVER feel overwhelmed when you think about all the wrongs in the world? I think those of us who are high on care/harm are at risk of compassion fatigue. This is exacerbated by the media that know what our biases are and play on them. We allow ourselves to be manipulated.

Now that you know what your biases are, take a step back. When you read an article you would normally read, how do you feel? Can you detach? When I realized that my emotions were being deliberately played with in order to sell newspapers or advertising, I felt dismayed.

As we discussed in the care/harm chapter, stories feature individual victims instead of statistics exactly because the stories inflame emotions, but numbers don't. I don't want arousal that someone creates to drive my decision-making or my mental state. Just that awareness and intention can change your perspective, it did for me.

This is one way to mitigate this potential influence.

STEP 3: EXPLORE HOW THE OTHER SIDE'S ETHICAL ZONES ARE ACTIVE IN YOUR LIFE

IN STEP 1, you discovered you are stronger in certain areas. That doesn't mean you don't have the other areas at all, they just aren't as robust. In this step, I want you to spend time thinking about how and when you feel when you use the other Ethical Zones.

Here are some questions that you could ask yourself for each of the zones. Focus on those that you probably aren't as strong on. More exercises to help with this can be found in the separate *Persuade, Don't Preach Workbook*.

Belonging and Community Ethical Zone

- How much time do you spend online with people versus in person?
- Which make you feel better in terms of energy and feeling of connectedness? (The research shows that people feel more connected with in-person interactions than online interactions. Is that true for you?)
- Think about what groups you belong to. Are those groups online or in person? How do you feel about each of them?
- Did you used to belong to other groups but have dropped them? Why did you drop them? What do you miss about being in that group? What makes you glad you dropped the group?
- What can you do to help strengthen a group that you belong to?
- Think about joining other in-person groups that help people, combining belonging and caring.

Respect for Authority Ethical Zone

- Who do you admire? Who do you follow on Instagram, Twitter, or Facebook? Do you see all the movies or shows that certain actors are in? Do you follow certain sports figures? Do you buy clothes or makeup that certain influencers or bloggers use or recommend?
- Are there any people you used to admire but don't? Why did you drop them?
- Are there brands you trust and brands you don't? Why? What happened?
- Which news commentators do you admire and trust? Which

ones don't you trust? Why? How does that change the news you consume?

- Are there any people on the other side that you admire, even though you don't agree with them? Why or why not?

Sacredness/Purity Ethical Zone

- What makes you feel safe?
- What do you think is disgusting?
- How does this change the food you eat? The products you use?
- How do you feel about messiness and cleanliness? Do you get into conflicts with people who feel differently? Differences in this Ethical Zone may be at the root of the conflict. Can you see their point of view after reading the book so far?

Fairness Ethical Zone

- Which flavor of fairness do you prefer? Are you merit based or equality based? Or do you favor giving more to those who have been historically disadvantaged?
- Do you ever use the other form? How about inside your family? Or in your workplace?
- Do you get upset when someone cuts in line ahead of you when you have spent time waiting?
- How do you feel if a company says, "Everyday low pricing?" Does that mean you can trust their price?
- How about when you pay the same price for large cup of coffee as someone else pays for a small cup?
- How do you feel about the salaries of executives? Are they ever justified?
- Do you believe that increasing the minimum wage will help people? Does it matter if the company will go out of business if they have to increase salaries?
- Should companies that invest lots of money in research and development of new products be able to charge whatever they want for products?
- Should people who work harder than others be paid more?

Care/Harm Ethical Zone

- Does someone in your life get more concern than others? Think family and close friends, even work colleagues.
- Do you see the humanity in others, even if they aren't in your group? Or are you tempted to see them as less than human?

STEP 4: PRACTICE VALUING EQUALITY AND DIVERSITY

IF YOU ARE part of the Liberal choir, you probably hold beliefs in equality and diversity. Make it real in your life. Don't look down on others, don't be condescending. It's a common perception of Conservatives that Liberals are talking down to them. Don't provide them with ammunition. Even if you have much more education than the people you are talking to, you aren't any better than they are.

You may be aware that diversity is said to lead to better decision-making. We often think of this in terms of gender and race. Companies with women on their boards of directors are believed to do better financially.

But there's more to it than that. We need diversity of thought to get away from group think. One academic study demonstrated that diverse teams had better solutions to the problems, even though the participants rated the process as more uncomfortable when they were with a stranger. Diversity isn't easy, but it is valuable.

TV personality Van Jones appreciates the value of diversity. In a short series of his on CNN in 2017, *The Messy Truth with Van Jones*, he traveled around the US showcasing the diversity of real Americans. He followed that up with a book, *Beyond the Messy Truth*, in which he makes a case for appreciating the value of what both Conservatives and Liberals bring— that we need the balance of different ways of looking at how the world works.

Without both, he says we will go off track. I agree that we need to bring both perspectives together to get back on track.

A folk tale from India illustrates the value of paying attention to other viewpoints. Six blind men were given the opportunity to touch an elephant. Each touched a different part of the elephant; the one who touched the trunk thought the elephant was a snake; the one who touched its side thought it was a wall; and the one who touched its legs thought it was tree trunk. All of them had some truth to what they believed, but because their experiences were different, they all had different pieces of the truth. We need all the pieces of the truth that we can get.

STEP 5: ASSUME GOOD INTENTIONS

WE MAKE VALUE-LADEN pronouncements such as calling an act immoral, saying to vote your conscience, implying that we are more moral than they are or that our conscience is the only one that matters. We vilify the other side and "cancel" them. We might even call them evil.

I hope from reading Part I that you have a better opinion of the other side than you did before. Recognize that what gets reported in the news is the extremes, not the majority. It wouldn't be news if it was the majority. Don't assume everyone belongs to the extremes. Usually, the majority isn't evil, they don't think what they are proposing is immoral, and they are voting their conscience. Their conscience is just different than yours, and many other people around the world share their perspective.

This step brings up a philosophical question of whether humans can be all good or all evil, which is the question of duality. While some people may be all evil (for example, Hitler), most humans have both positive and negative bits. We don't want to admit the bad parts of ourselves, the parts that we are ashamed of.

A common way to deal with our own negative traits is to ignore them, but they end up popping up as traits of the other side. This means that the items that so upset us in other people are issues that are often true for us on some level. This is what psychologists call projection.

As the ancient Chinese philosopher/poet Seng-Ts'an said:

> Do not search for the truth; only cease to cherish opinions.
> Do not hold to dualistic views, avoid such habits carefully.
> If there is even a trace of right and wrong, the mind is lost in confusion.

There are two parts to assume good intentions: One is to first deal with your issues, especially any shame you feel about not being perfect. You need to unwire the hot buttons you have. Both therapy and work on a

12 step program can be very helpful at dealing with shame. I also found Brené Brown's book *The Gifts of Imperfection* helpful.

Another way to address this is to do things to expand your own altruistic side. What we pay attention to increases. Some possible techniques to expand your better angels side are doing altruistic acts, creating gratitude lists, and promoting spiritual practices, including meditation, spiritual literature, and worship services. Note: This does not work if you expect a reward for your altruism; your motives matter.

You need to do these acts to become a better person. This is the question that TV show *The Good Place* dealt with. While philosophers may doubt that is possible, I disagree. I believe it is possible. We want to reform prisoners. Addicts and alcoholics who practice a 12 step program are said to be recovered. In religion, we call that redemption. Presumably, even Hitler had a positive part of his personality early in his life, but didn't pay attention to it, so it withered.

Now that you are aware of your own imperfections, when you look at the other side, recognize that they have the same issues that you do and try to assume that, just like you, you both want the best.

Van Jones is a terrific example of someone who was able to look to the other side to provide help that his side couldn't provide to work on an issue he cared deeply about. Because he assumed good intentions and valued what the other side could bring, his efforts to pass the First Step Act for Prison Reform was successfully passed with support from both sides of the political aisle in late 2018. This has had a tremendous impact on the men and women who have been released from prison.

STEP 6: ASSUME YOU CAN LEARN FROM THE OTHER SIDE

WE ARE SO caught up in vilifying the other side that we don't pay attention to the fact that they probably have some valid points.

A Malay proverb captures what happens when we don't pay attention to the other viewpoint: "Clapping with the right hand only will not produce a noise."

Podcasters Sarah Stewart Holland and Beth Silvers talk about the realities they learned that contradicted their in-going assumptions when they opened themselves up to hearing facts and learning about the other side.

It's brave to do that. As I discussed, the Ethical Zone of understanding is one in which we have no attachment to any point of view and awareness of all points of view.

This is otherwise known as humility. Don't think of it as humiliation, but humility. It's a virtue. Really. Otherwise you are self-righteous and smug. That's not pretty. Instead, be brave. Like Yoda who said, "Many of the truths that we cling to depend on our point of view."

STEP 7: BE PEACEFUL

A WISE PERSON once told me that activists work by bringing violence from one area into another, even if they change it from physical violence to emotional violence.

I was told this when I described what was going on at a college campus as a result of the BDS movement. (BDS stands for boycott, divestment, and sanctions. It asks colleges to divest the stock of companies that they view as taking the Israeli side of the Palestinian/Israeli conflict.)

The local BDS chapter's tactics were to try to pressure the student body to force the administrations and the trustees to divest certain stocks. They were creating chaos, including making Jewish students feel unwelcome at the campus. When confronted about the atmosphere they were creating, they said it didn't matter because all that mattered was the violence to the Palestinians. But emotional violence doesn't bring peace. Only peace creates peace.

As part of this process, deal with any emotional violence that you may be tempted to enact before you enter into an encounter. Clean up your own issues first. Go back to step 4 for help if you are stuck.

As the Dalai Lama has said: "If we ourselves remain angry and then sing world peace, it has little meaning. First, our individual self must learn peace. This we can practice. Then we can teach the rest of the world."

STEP 8: FIND A TRIBE TO SUPPORT YOU

IT'S EASY TO join a mob that cancels someone. As I talked about in the belonging and community chapter, you are influenced by the people you identify with and spend time with. It's tough to go out on your own. The tribe you identify with may not be supportive on this path. For example,

Van Jones has been vilified by progressives for working with Conserva- tives on his successful path to getting the First Step Act for Prison Reform passed.

You won't be able to continue on this path if you don't find a group that will encourage you on this path, to encourage you to think well of the other person. This has to be a new type of tribe, with special characteris- tics. A later chapter will help you identify the characteristics of the tribe so you will know if you already have one, or if you need to find a new one.

This Midrash quote captures the strength of the group: "Separate reeds are weak and easily broken; but bound together they are strong and hard to tear apart."

This can be a church group or a group of friends. Or you could use my closed online Facebook group, "Persuade, Don't Preach," to find the support you need if you can't find an in-person group. Also watching and listening to shows by people like Van Jones, Sarah Stewart Holland, and Beth Silvers who are doing this type of work can also provide support. See a list of organizations that may be helpful in the appendix.

STEP 9: REVIEW THE ETHICAL ZONES FOR THE ISSUE YOU WANT TO ADDRESS

IN THE PREVIOUS section, I analyzed the major issues of the day by the Ethical Zones that are activated when we talk about them.

Pick one issue and go back and identify which position is yours and which is likely to be the position of someone you will disagree with. You will need that in your conversation. You also want to think about what is important to you and review any facts and figures so you have them avail- able to yourself in the conversation.

STEP 10: DECIDE ON YOUR BOUNDARIES

DECIDE ON WHAT the boundaries of this are for you. In her book *Brav- ing the Wilderness*, Brené Brown reported that people who were success- ful in these types of difficult conversations set boundaries where they would not listen to dehumanizing language. That's because that is what they needed to feel safe in the conversation.

Start with that premise and then figure out what your personal boundaries are. Don't make them too rigid, or too inclusive, because the point of this conversation is to allow people to make comments that you will disagree with. This conversation may not be easy, and you need to be able to listen to challenging ideas.

Questions to ask yourself include these: Have you ever had beliefs that were challenged? How did you feel? How did you react? Can you figure out a way to detach from the challenge so that you can participate in this conversation without reacting negatively?

STEP 11: PRACTICE IN A SUPPORTIVE SETTING

THIS IS DIFFICULT work. Before you try it out for real, practice in a setting where you feel comfortable: the tribe I suggest you create in step 8. The workshops that I offer also provide a short-term tribe that will enable you to rehearse these challenging conversations and feel more prepared.

STEP 12: CHOOSE A PERSON TO TRY THIS WITH

CHOOSE A PERSON you are in a relationship with but with whom you have already had a difficult conversation about issues. Or choose someone you haven't had the conversation with because you think you know that you will disagree with them. Don't choose someone just to influence them or choose someone whose views are so extreme that they won't be able to deal with your boundaries (for example, they believe certain people ought to be killed).

Choose someone you admire in some way; don't choose someone you despise. Choose someone you want to develop a relationship with more fully, but also someone whose views are not too extreme.

15

HOW TO PERSUADE ON AN INDIVIDUAL LEVEL

S O FAR, THIS book has focused on how and why we are polarized, why preaching from our beliefs doesn't work, and the kind of preparation you need in order to do this work. Are you discouraged?

In this era where we recognize the polarization of beliefs, we can feel hopeless that life will ever change. After all, these beliefs that this book has been discussing feel overwhelming because people aren't thinking about them. They are just acting on previously held beliefs. We may get discouraged because people seem so irrational to us sometimes, and we may have tried to convince someone and just made the situation worse. As we learned, this may be due to the high need for cognitive closure that some people have.

We avoid these conversations. We keep exchanges on a superficial level thinking that is safe. But it doesn't help us heal what is going on. We are frozen, individually and as a society. We aren't changing, we aren't growing. We aren't doing anything except getting upset.

But there is hope that life can be different. The rest of this book is practical, actually a how-to guide that explains how to persuade. I am drawing on several methods that have been developed that have successfully persuaded people. Most of these techniques rely in some way on keeping people's minds open, attempting to counteract a high need for cognitive closure.

In this section of the book, I will tell you how to use what you have just learned to have more productive conversations and give more productive speeches and presentations. Even with people you disagree with. Especially with people you disagree with.

Here are the steps:

Set Intention with the Other Person and Ask Permission

Here's some language that might help you start a different type of conversation: "I want to have a different type of conversation with you about the issues of the day. I want to truly understand things from your perspective, so to do that I need to ask a lot of questions. This is a touchy area and it's a new way of talking about it, so I might not do it perfectly. I beg your indulgence and ask you to be gentle with me as we do this conversation. Is this okay to go ahead? Is now a good time?"

You can practice this approach and make it your own.

State Your Boundaries

As I talked about in step 10 of the previous chapter, setting boundaries is crucial to your feeling safe.

Here's some potential language for how to do this, but you need to practice and find your own: "Before we start, I want to say that there are some things that I need in order to feel safe in this conversation. If we can't stick to those rules, I will have to stop the conversation if they happen. For me what is important is that people need to be talked about as human beings and not animals or insects. Can we agree that we both will not use negative language?"

Listen Differently

Most persuasion techniques start with a listening phase. After all, you need to know where your audience is coming from so you can bring them along, right? But there are problems with that. One is that humans think faster than we talk, so we may get impatient listening. I know I am guilty of that. I used to fill in time doing mindless activities on the sly while listening to meandering discussions.

But I have learned that it is important to be totally present. If you aren't, the person you are listening to will sense it and will experience it as a lack of respect. That means no cell phones, no texting, no playing games on my phone like I used to do. You can approach it as a meditation by paying attention to your breathing and any emotions that come up for you. You should also pay attention to the other person's stance, their body language, and their emotions.

Another problem is our reactions. I can't tell you the number of times I have heard people say that they try to listen to people they disagree with, but their blood pressure goes up and they start thinking about how they are going to respond, and all the high-minded intention of active listening goes out the window. That's why the last chapter was how to prepare yourself. You are taking a different type of action than your usual and you need to practice. That's why I recommend workshop training.

Ask Questions

Start by asking questions to understand the values. Here's a starter question: "What's important to you about this issue?"

Use the information in the first two sections of the book to identify which Ethical Zones come up. Ask a confirming question to make sure that you are right. You might phrase the question in the following way: "Do I hear that the value of x is important to you on the issue of y?"

Then probe, perhaps with simple questions like, "Tell me more" or with specific questions like "In what way does the value apply in this situation?" After you have probed the first Ethical Zone, move on to the others that you heard being referenced in your conversation and ask questions about that one.

At some point, when appropriate, pick up on a comment they made and say, "I admire that about you." Of course, only say this if it is true. No toadying or bullshitting, we need to be real.

You can also mention: "I realize that the value of x is important, and I have been looking at where it applies in my own life. For example, [fill this with an idea from step 9 in the previous chapter]." Again, only if it is true.

Reframing

Finally, we get to reframing. The chapter that follows explains reframing in detail and gives examples, but, in brief, reframing is using a value that is important to the person you are talking with but tying it to the issue in an unexpected and relevant way.

You might refer to a previous comment, such as: "I know loyalty to our country is important to you. But I am confused about how that relates to the fact that [and fill in the blank with a relevant fact]."

This technique has been shown to be extremely effective at changing people's opinions. You are telling them that their values are important and then getting them to think about applying them in a new way.

Caution: It will be tempting to revert to your values and the typical way you talk about an issue. Don't do it! It won't work and will bring you back to the same predictable arguments that you always have or avoid.

> *Reframing has been shown to be extremely effective at changing people's opinions. You are telling them that their values are important and then getting them to think about applying them in a new way.*

Review

You are almost there. You just need to review and see where you are. Has the person changed at all? If so, summarize the conversation and note the change. If not, then go back to asking more questions. As the shampoo directions say, rinse and repeat. Perhaps you need to use a different Ethical Zone.

Closing

When you are done, or perhaps just tired, you need to thank the person for their time and attention. They have given you a gift of themselves. Be appreciative.

OTHER TECHNIQUES

ALTHOUGH THESE AREN'T core to this technique, they have been shown to be effective in other research and may be useful in the conversation. I've included these techniques because sometimes you need something besides reframing. Practice the following techniques so you can use them at your discretion.

Deep Canvassing

This technique has been demonstrated to be effective in changing people's opinions on the issue of transgender rights. It has also been used in a campaign for gay rights, but the research that studied it was flawed, so we only have one proven case study.

Key to this technique is developing a personal connection. Ask questions like, "How has this issue touched your own life? Do you know any people who are ___?"

After the person has opened up and you have demonstrated that you care about how their experiences have been, the canvasser is then able to share what is important to them. By highlighting our common humanity, this builds bridges between people.

More details of deep canvassing can be found here: https://callhub.io/deep-canvassing/.

Illusion of Explanatory Depth Challenge

Another technique relates to the idea that most people hold views from their values and not from the facts, which is a cognitive psychology factor called the illusion of explanatory depth.

Here's how the technique has been tested, using a zipper example:

1. On a scale from 1 to 7, how well do you understand how zippers work?
2. How does a zipper work? Describe in as much detail as you can all the steps involved in a zipper's operation.
3. Now, on the same 1 to 7 scale, rate your knowledge of how a zipper works again.

When people go through this process, they realize that they really don't know that much. Let's see how this could be applied in a situation about a social or political issue.

1. Start with acknowledging the passion that this person has about this issue.
2. Then ask how knowledgeable they are about the issue. It feels

too formal to ask them to rate their knowledge, so don't do that.

3. Then ask them to explain how the issue works in detail. Say you are curious to learn more about how it works. Use probes such as "Can you explain this to me more fully? Maybe you need a paper and pencil to draw a diagram." Because most people don't actually know how objects work in detail, they may get flustered. You need to encourage them to do the best they can.

What you are actually doing here is helping people to move out of the Ethical Zones that were dominating their thinking and into the rationality Ethical Zone. This is exactly what Sarah Stewart Holland and Beth Silvers have been pushing themselves to do in their podcast. They acknowledge that they really didn't know the facts, they just thought they did.

This could be of most use in areas in which the perceptions that people have are radically inaccurate, like the data on immigration. It doesn't work to lecture people on the correct data but making them realize that they actually don't know what they are talking about works. But be careful not to be condescending. Keep in mind that they have to realize on their own that they don't know the facts.

Any of these conversations will take time. The deep canvassing technique, which I have borrowed some of these steps from, is estimated to hold conversations at twenty minutes or so. But I have added steps, so I estimate that these conversations will take at least thirty minutes. But if they work, then they are worth it, aren't they? And you have built a connection to someone you have been avoiding until now. And maybe, just maybe, we will start to heal the rifts in our society if we all have respectful, empathetic conversations like this, one person at a time.

16
THE ETHICAL FRAMES PERSUASION TECHNIQUE: REFRAMING

THIS BOOK HAS focused on getting you to understand how and why other people think like they do. It has discussed the way the associations have been made between issues and the Ethical Zones. Both Liberals and Conservatives tie their most important Ethical Zones to certain issues.

The premise of reframing is that no issue is inextricably linked to an Ethical Zone. Almost every issue can be viewed through a number of different Ethical Zones. Changing the interpretation of the issue by switching Ethical Zones can work to change people's minds on a particular issue. Figuring out how to change the Ethical Zone that is associated with an issue is tricky, but it can be done once you have reached the Ethical Zone of understanding.

The rules for reframing are that you need to use an Ethical Zone that is strong for the target audience, is relevant to the issue, but is not currently used to support the issue.

Academics Robb Willer and Matt Feinberg, who created this groundbreaking technique, have done a number of studies demonstrating that reframing is effective at changing people's minds on issues. They have demonstrated the technique on five different societal issues:

- Increased MILITARY SPENDING was supported by more Liberals when framed using the need-based flavor of fairness (that the military increases opportunities for disadvantaged populations who are more likely to be in the military) than when it was framed using belonging, a Conservative Ethical Zone.

- Universal HEALTHCARE was supported by significantly more Conservatives when the sacredness Ethical Zone (sick people are disgusting) was used than when an equality-flavored fairness Ethical Zone argument was used.
- SAME-SEX MARRIAGE was supported by more Conservatives when it was framed using belonging-based arguments than when it was framed using fairness arguments and more than when it was not framed at all.
- Liberals were more likely to support making ENGLISH the official language of the US when it was framed as a fairness issue than when it was framed as a belonging issue.
- Conservatives were more likely to support ENVIRONMENTAL issues when they were framed using the sacredness Ethical Zone than when they supported using the care/harm Ethical Zone.

Robb Willer's excellent TEDxMarin talk on reframing can be found at https://www.ted.com/talks/robb_willer_how_to_have_better_political_conversations.

> *The rules for reframing are that you need to use an Ethical Zone that is strong for the target audience, is relevant to the issue, but is not currently used to support the issue.*

I have found several examples of successful reframing in the real world:

- The Texas antilittering campaign is the best example of using the belonging and community Ethical Zone in the real world. It has run for thirty years and has been effective in decreasing littering in Texas. In it, the Texas Department of Transportation ties not littering with being a Texan. They have a website (http://www.dontmesswithtexas.org/) where you can see the various iterations of the successful campaign.
- A campaign for recycling in Conservative Utah that I

discovered on a trip to Utah may have been created by someone familiar with Willer and Feinberg's work. The banner for the Brigham Young Physical Facilities unit promotes recycling with the line "Respect for our sacred resources" just like one of the Willer/Feinberg studies.

- A century ago life insurance was regarded as disgusting because it was associated with death (a prime example of violating the sacredness Ethical Zone) but has been reframed to be about caring for your family after you are gone (using the care/harm Ethical Zone), which has totally changed customers' reactions.

- As I illustrated in the deep dive into Conservatives chapter, it seems to me that the issue of gay rights has advanced because the issue moved from the care/harm and fairness Ethical Zones favored by Liberals (people deserve to love who they wish) to one that touched on a Conservative hot button, the family, which touches both the belonging and sacredness Ethical Zones (Gays should be able to marry and form families.). This reframing also avoids triggering the disgust reaction to the violation of the sacredness Ethical Zone.

- A story I heard from someone about a small town in upstate New York illustrates another way belonging can be used to reframe. This town held a beauty contest in which a young Muslim girl had enrolled, but she couldn't participate in the swimsuit portion of the contest because of her religion. Although the belonging and sacredness Ethical Zones could have easily led to her rejection, that didn't happen. Instead, the town rallied around her and allowed her to participate because "she's one of us." It's amazing how flexible the belonging and community Ethical Zone can be; her Muslim otherness could have been used against her, but it wasn't. Instead, she was embraced as one of the community.

- There is an attempt to get firefighters to wear protective masks, which goes against the macho firefighter culture (a belonging Ethical Zone). The reframing is using the phrase "clean is the new cool," which invokes the sacredness Ethical Zone.

- A pro-life campaign, "Real Men Love Babies," attempts to redefine masculinity using the belonging Ethical Zone, instead of the Ethical Zones that are usually invoked about the issue of abortion, care/harm and sacredness.

17

HOW REFRAMING MIGHT HELP PERSUADE

I'VE GIVEN A lot of thought and creative energy to how reframing might help with the various issues I have talked about in this book. Here are some ideas for each of the issues that I spoke about, with some potential solutions to try. Some might work, and some might not, but we need to try. There also could be others; these are just a start.

Please feel free to use or adapt these and to try your own. I hope that reaching the Ethical Zone of understanding will have released a lot of creativity.

> *I hope that reaching the Ethical Zone of understanding will have released a lot of creativity.*

GUN CONTROL

EARLIER, I CONCLUDED that violations of two Ethical Zones contributed to the negative reactions among Conservatives: belonging and community (being an American means owning a gun) and sacredness (a gun has taken on a mythical importance).

I also think that guns mean safety to Conservatives—another part of the sacredness zone, exactly opposite to what Liberals believe. Plus, elements of the respect for authority Ethical Zone are also involved, as are concepts of masculinity (another part of belonging).

This makes guns one of the issues most tightly tied to Ethical Zones and the most challenging. Anyone who wants to address this issue needs to really understand the qualities of these Ethical Zones and how to use them to reframe.

Here are some thoughts on how reframing might be used to address the issue of gun control.

- What definitely won't work is an emphasis on one of the Liberal Ethical Zones, care/harm. Conservatives know that Liberals feel this way, so it is a tip-off that the message isn't talking to them if there is a focus on the care/harm Ethical Zone. Therefore, a gun-control campaign that implies that guns kill people won't work. Conservatives feel guns are safe and they have more experience of them being safe than unsafe. Familiarity makes people feel things are safe.
- A gun-control effort could use the fairness Ethical Zone. Fairness is more often a Liberal Ethical Zone, but Conservatives do care about it, just in a different way than Liberals—the merit-based flavor. By using a merit-flavored fairness Ethical Zone, you might be able to persuade Conservatives. This is similar to where the NRA used to be before they become more extreme. There are a few possibilities:

  - You can preserve the rights of gun owners by restricting gun sales to people who endanger that right.
  - Or the right to own guns needs to be earned by responsible gun use.
  - What might be even more powerful is to tie responsible gun ownership and use to being a real American. Phrases like: "Real Americans don't shoot innocent children" and "Real Americans don't shoot families at church" would tie both the belonging Ethical Zone (American) and the sacredness Ethical Zone (innocent children and families at church) to the belonging and community Ethical Zone.

- New Zealand Prime Minister Jacinda Ardern effectively used the belonging and community Ethical Zone when she said of the victims of the Christchurch shooting, "They are us."

- You might also be able to stretch that tie to address the problems of guns being used in suicide and children getting to guns that aren't locked up:

  - "Real Americans don't shoot themselves when things look down; they get help." (This might be able to counteract some of the male stereotypes that men don't ask for help when they feel depressed if it could be tied to patriotism to ask for help.)
  - "Real Americans make sure their children can't get to guns until they are old enough to use them responsibly." (This might be able to counter the belief that children won't touch guns if they are told not to.)

- If an authority figure was available to say that guns need to be locked up, that could work. Unfortunately, the current president is not likely to do that, given the support he has from the NRA.

The NRA has been a powerful lobby that promoted unrestricted gun rights, but it has been weakened. Now might be an opportune time to challenge them. The NRA used to be more moderate and talk about responsibility. That might also be a useful idea to reference.

ANTIVACCINE

THE LOWERED PERCENTAGE of children being vaccinated is leading to sporadic epidemics of preventable illnesses, such as measles. As I mentioned in the health chapter, the mothers who are antivaxxers appear to be both low in respect for authority and high in sacredness. Thus, a campaign with a doctor or a vaccine company or government won't work. What can be done?

Here are some persuasion ideas drawn from knowledge of the Ethical Zones:

- For those mothers who are Liberal, the most successful campaign idea might be to use both the care/harm and fairness Ethical Zones to talk about the disadvantaged children who have chronic illnesses who would die if they get the measles (the need flavor of fairness), and that vaccination of all children is the way to protect them.
- These mothers are high in sacredness (even if they are Liberal), so a campaign about how disgusting the actual illnesses are could work. This could be indirect, by focusing on emerging illnesses such as the Zika and CoVid-19 viruses. Remember, disgustingness is a powerful emotional motivator.
- Although these mothers are low in respect for authority overall so a campaign by doctors won't work, they do have some people they hold in high regard. Finding mothers who fit that profile and highlighting that they decided to vaccinate their child (perhaps combining that messenger with one of the other messages) could be successful.
- Finally, although the levels of belonging tend to be low among the Liberal women, a campaign that presented vaccination as the choice of socially responsible mothers (as Liberals would like to see themselves) might work, especially if combined with another message.

Again, no one knows if these particular strategies would work, but it does provide some ideas for how the reframing technique can work for this issue.

HEALTHCARE

OF ALL OF the issues, I think the divide on healthcare could be successfully bridged more easily than some of these other issues because it isn't tied tightly to an Ethical Zone.

Willer and Feinberg demonstrated how reframing can be used to increase support of healthcare for all by using the sacredness Ethical Zone. Their particular wording was that "sick people are disgusting." But I think it could be even stronger if words about "infections" were also used.

Everyone will want to stop the spread of disease, especially those who are higher on the sacredness/purity Ethical Zone. And they specifically will want to keep their tribe safe, so wording like "keep the people you love safe from disgusting infections that could spread by making sure that everyone has healthcare" could be a powerful message.

IMMIGRATION AND RACE

LIKE GUN CONTROL, this area is also difficult. But that doesn't mean it is impossible.

Similar to gun control, tying the merit-based flavor of the fairness Ethical Zone to immigration might work to convince Conservatives.

One way is to take advantage of the fact of how difficult it is to immigrate to America. One possible reframing could be: America, a place you are either born to or you have to earn. Earning could be by the difficulties that they faced, or the rigors that the State Department used to vet potential immigrants.

There have been other cases where people who have worked for the US have earned the right to come to the US, which could be another way to prove how difficult it is. Other times, immigrants have earned the right to stay in the US by enlisting in the military.

I found another use of the merit-based flavor of the fairness Ethical Zone in a comment by Travis Tranel, a Wisconsin Republican state representative who has proposed bringing immigrants "who want to work hard" to help repopulate rural areas of Wisconsin. This has potential.

Descendants of enslaved people represent a different case. They are citizens. Naming them as Americans could be useful, using the belonging and community Ethical Zone. Further, saying that they and their ancestors have contributed to the American way of life (a merit-flavored fairness argument) might also work.

Another relevant fact about people of color is that they are more likely to serve in our armed forces. This could also be used as the basis of a merit flavor reframing, that their service has earned them respect. I realize that this would be abhorrent to Liberals, but it could work with Conservatives, especially because it would access the patriotism of the belonging and community Ethical Zone.

ABORTION

NOTE THAT MOST people's views on abortion are nuanced. Pro-life and pro-choice are simplistic, too simplistic to accurately represent the views of the majority. The extremes do not represent the bulk of people's opinions.

I found applying the concept of reframing to abortion challenging. Even though I have been working on it for years, I don't have a recommendation. What I do recommend is using one of the other techniques (deep canvassing and the illusion of explanatory depth challenge) to address abortion as described in chapter 17. That's why I included them, despite the fact that they don't really fit with most of the book. I wanted to provide you with at least some tools to address this very difficult area.

HOMOSEXUALITY AND QUEERNESS

THE GAY RIGHTS movement switch to using gay marriage was a masterful way to use the reframing technique and has successfully improved attitudes toward gays.

Willer and Feinberg's research provided another example of how to use reframing, by using the belonging and community Ethical Zone. Still another technique (deep canvassing) has also been proven to successfully improve attitudes toward trans people. I also wonder if an effort that talked about the diversity of how God made us might be a useful, complementary way to utilize the sacredness Ethical Zone in a way that would appeal to Conservatives.

CLIMATE CHANGE AND GLOBAL WARMING

I GET FRUSTRATED by the climate change activists who continue on the path of talking about destruction of the earth but ignore the sacredness/purity Ethical Zone that would help them gain support if they used it.

Willer and Feinberg have proven that such reframing works in their research. It was so powerful that even though the message in their research didn't mention climate change, Conservatives changed their attitudes about climate change. The technique has been used before in a previous environmental campaign.

When I was in Utah, I saw several ad campaigns that the Mormons were doing using the latest social science research, including a campaign for recycling at Brigham Young University that used sacredness that I described earlier. It seems so obvious to me, but the activists are so caught up in their own Ethical Zones that they can't see the benefit of appealing to those who have different values. All that needs to be done is to revive the "Keep America Beautiful" campaign or any campaign focused on pure air and water. That's it! It's simple and everyone would get what they want.

18
REFRAMING
PRESIDENT TRUMP

THIS BOOK HAS demonstrated the clear differences in moral founda-tions/Ethical Zones between Conservatives and Liberals.

What doesn't work in convincing Conservatives is to rely on the two moral foundations that Liberals are high on, care/harm and the equality-based flavor of fairness. For example, the outrage over the inhumane treat-ment of child immigrants on the border has gone as far as it can in convincing people that the Trump administration is cruel. It was effective among moderates and among female Conservatives, who are higher in the care/harm Ethical Zone than male Conservatives.

As one woman interviewed by a FiveThirtyEight.com reporter said, the Trump supporters feel the need to dehumanize those children, saying that because their parents were illegal immigrants, they didn't deserve bet-ter treatment. (Do you hear the violations of the belonging and sacredness Ethical Zones being invoked, as well as the merit-based flavor fairness?)

Similarly, the indignation over the Muslim ban, with families being broken up, has probably done as much damage to the Trump image as it is going to. Liberals can't rely on the care/harm Ethical Zone to defeat Trump—that's preaching. They need to persuade by using unexpected but relevant Conservative moral values.

THE NEVER TRUMPERS

LET'S LOOK AT two sources for how to appeal to this group: the Never Trumpers and the academic research. Then I will weigh in with other ideas.

President Trump has branded people who disagree with him as Never Trumpers and called them "human scum" in a tweet, evoking the sacredness/purity moral foundation. Some former Never Trumpers appear to have been won over by some Conservative wins such as the tax cut, regulatory rollback, and Conservative judge appointments. Some of these are economic Conservative positions, but the Conservative judge appointments are focused on the abortion issue. The sacredness Ethical Zone as it relates to pregnancy is a very strong motivator for Conservatives.

Other Never Trumpers have left the Republican party. But there are those who continue to stay as Republicans and oppose the president because of his lies, his alleged corruption, his admiration for strongmen like Vladimir Putin, and his unpredictability.

One prominent Never Trumper stated that although President Trump's attention to Conservative causes is causing short-term wins, it is at the expense of the long-term viability of Conservative values. Further, he expressed embarrassment of how President Trump is perceived by other world leaders, leading to loss of status for the US. These are all centered on issues about respect for authority (lack of predictability, lack of trust, and loss of face among other world leaders shake this Ethical Zone) and the patriotism form of belonging.

After the House of Representatives voted to impeach the president, in December 2019, *Christianity Today* (a leading Christian publication founded by Billy Graham but which is no longer associated with the Graham family) came out against President Trump citing Trump's immoral actions in business and with women, his abuse of power, his lies and lack of loyalty to the constitution.

Note the use of the word *immoral* to describe the lack of loyalty to the country, and the violation of the sacredness Ethical Zone. They also pointed out the conflict that Evangelical Trump supporters have been ignoring between different violations of the Ethical Zones: supporters concentrate on the issue of abortion as evil (a violation of the sacredness Ethical Zone) while ignoring other violations.

ACADEMIC RESEARCH

AT LEAST THREE sets of academic researchers have pinpointed ways to win over (or at least shake the conviction of) at least some of President Trump's base. Robb Willer and a student, Jan Voekel, conducted experiments to determine if a Democratic candidate that evokes Conservative values but has Liberal policy positions would be successful among Conservative voters. The answer is yes. So that's one technique Democrats could use.

During the 2016 election, Voekel and Matt Feinberg conducted experiments about moral reframing for both presidential candidates. The Hillary Clinton study was inconclusive, but the Trump study showed that highlighting Trump's lack of patriotism (he evaded the draft, has put his own interests ahead of the country's) was effective at reducing support among Conservatives, but not with moderates.

Three researchers at the University of Maryland have also done a study that showed another way that President Trump has a weakness. If voters were told that President Trump wasn't a self-made man, that he inherited his wealth and didn't earn it, that weakened support as well. This shakes one of the pillars of the respect for authority Ethical Zone and also takes advantage of the merit-based flavor of fairness that Conservatives favor.

OTHER POSSIBILITIES

I THINK THERE are other ways that Ethical Zone reframing can be used to shake the hold that President Trump has on Conservatives. While the one academic study included one reference to patriotism, President Trump has taken a lot of actions that could be perceived as unpatriotic. Our military is well respected by Conservatives, and President Trump attempts to boost himself in their eyes by visiting the troops overseas. But he has fired several well-respected generals who have been on his staff and overturned current army command's ruling on several war crimes rulings.

Being in the military requires putting your country over your own well-being, a key part of patriotism. I think that is a question that could be raised by President Trump's opponents in a lot of different ways that might be successful because it plays on a key area for Conservatives. Conservatives have a great deal of respect for the military and provide a lot of the personnel in the armed forces. Showing disrespect for the chain of command might sow some doubt.

What is surprising to me is that many Never Trumpers don't cite some of the other inconsistencies between Conservative values and President Trump's behavior. One obvious one is his demonstrated infidelity, a key violation of the sacredness/purity Ethical Zone that was cited by *Chris-*

tianity Today. But Liberals have eliminated any benefit they could have gotten because they focused on the harm to the women being used by President Trump, and not on the harm to the value of marriage.

> *I think a question (of loyalty) that could be raised by President Trump's opponents in a lot of different ways might be successful because it plays on a key area for Conservatives.*

While there are some indications that people who would otherwise value the sanctity of marriage are holding their nose and voting for President Trump despite that violation, they may be open to persuasion if there is a concerted effort to call out how President Trump violated his marital vows.

Another area of potential weakness for President Trump that relates to the Ethical Zones is change. Conservatives love consistency. President Trump's unpredictable nature as expressed in his tweets is a weakness as far as Conservatives are concerned. Conservatives often say that they like President Trump except for his tweets. This is a potential opening.

Winning in the global order could be another way to attack President Trump. The effect of losing to other countries could awaken a shared sense of belonging and of patriotism.

Finally, if Conservatives start believing that they can't trust President Trump to tell the truth, that may shake their belief in him as a trustworthy authority figure. They need an authority figure to tell the truth because of their high need for cognitive closure. That's a tricky one, however, because they are not going to trust Liberal sources about what is true. The *Christianity Today* editorial may have an impact.

These are all ideas that might work. Try them out in your conversations. Modify them as it occurs to you. Just don't use the expected Ethical Zones; you need to use an unexpected one for this technique to work.

19
CREATING A REFRAMING CAMPAIGN

T HE SAME TECHNIQUES that you can use in one-on-one conversations to build relationships can be used to create a campaign speech or grassroots canvassing instructions. This worked for the gay rights campaign and can work for you.

First, you need to create a message. Use the information in the previous chapters and any conversations you have had with potential audience members to test the effectiveness of the ideas. Remember, the key is to use a surprising Ethical Frame that isn't usually used for the issue but is relevant to the target audience. Then tie the Ethical Frame to the issue in a way that makes sense.

Second, you need to educate your advocates. You need a consistent message. As I heard the story, the gay rights campaign did exactly that in an email message that told volunteers exactly what to say and, importantly, what *not* to say. That's crucial, because unless you do that, your volunteers will default to their usual way of supporting their arguments. That won't convince anyone except the volunteers.

Third, I am going to suggest that you test your campaign. This technique has been tested academically and has real-life examples, and I believe that it will work, but that is not the same as a controlled test in the field. The deep canvassing campaign was tested in a test like that and has proven effective in the field.

> *To create a reframing campaign, you need to tell supporters what to say and what not to say.*

20
BUILDING A NEW TYPE
OF COMMUNITY

T HE EARLIER CHAPTER on the belonging and community Ethical Zone talked about the benefits and downsides to community. As I wrote in an earlier chapter, community and belonging are crucial to our well-being and to our identity. Without realizing, we shape-shift in order to feel as if we belong. We often choose our community without thinking about it, by proximity and by what feels comfortable.

But in order to be able to successfully do this new type of work, we need a different type of community. Otherwise, if we don't have a positive community that is supportive to this type of work, we run the risk of being derailed. As you work on applying these concepts, some will criticize you because they aren't there yet or they don't understand. Unless you have another source of support, you may never be able to accomplish the persuasion called for in the title of this book.

So instead of choosing a community by default, we need to think about what a community means to us and actively evaluate the communities we think we might want to belong to. Because this is a change, we don't have a lot of experience in this, so it is difficult. This chapter is intended to give you information to help gauge potential communities, not how to create one. The *Persuade, Don't Preach Leader's Guide* on how to form a supportive community will be published in fall 2020.

> *In order to be able to successfully do this new type of work,*
> *we need a different type of community.*

This has been the most difficult chapter for me to write because community is an intersection of our individual expectations and behavior, the behavior of those around us, and the community norms. There are no perfect communities because they are created by fragile human beings. The best you can do is to find one that is close.

Because no community is perfect, those among us who are damaged (and who isn't damaged, in one way or another?) may perceive all communities as threatening, even the healthiest ones. Conversely, wounded people may be attracted to a community that looks different superficially than abusive communities they have been a part of, but underneath repeats the same pattern. And injured people can set up a negative response pattern that repeats their bad experiences with community.

In a corollary to the saying "hurt people hurt people," I would add "damaged people create damaging communities" and "damaged people perceive damaging communities even if they aren't."

I remember talking to an accomplished woman in my spiritual community who is articulate when talking one-on-one but freezes in a group because of a bad experience in her former faith community. And I myself was damaged when I first came to my self-help group. Even though the group was a relatively healthy space, I didn't talk for years, I just hid. But gradually, over time, I grew healthier and healthier and have become a leader in it and in other communities.

Brené Brown, in her book about belonging, *Braving the Wilderness*, focuses on telling individuals the changes they need to make: to be brave, to be themselves and not conform. Certainly, resisting pressure to conform is important, and we may not even realize that we are doing it. That's why it's on my list. It takes listening to the still small voice inside of us, the one that says that something isn't right, to recognize when you are conforming but it isn't really what you believe or want to do. But communities that aren't supportive actively suppress your ability to communicate with that inner voice.

Brown also makes an important point: instead of looking for ways we don't belong, we need to look for ways that we do. This change in perspective has been a turning point for her and her children.

As I was contemplating writing this chapter, I was just going to summarize other people's work. But I realized that over the past ten years I have accumulated experience in being part of and in creating a new kind of community. I have been in leadership roles in creating a new organization, in running workshops and retreats, and in a spiritual community. Because I grew up not feeling like I belonged anywhere, this realization has represented a huge step forward for me. I haven't done it perfectly, but I have grown and look at the world quite differently now.

This chapter includes the lessons I have learned about what makes a community that is supportive of the type of challenging work that this book demands.

Bad Communities for Personal Growth	Good Communities for Personal Growth
Shames and/or ostracizes people for bad behavior.	Has a set of agreed-upon ground rules; names behavior as bad, not people; deals with disruptive behavior in a warm and loving manner.
Shames and/or ostracizes people for mistakes. Comparison and judgment of others is expected.	Recognizes that this work is hard, mistakes are forgiven and celebrates progress. Empathy is practiced.
Pressures people to conform; requires certain beliefs and behavior. May use time pressure.	Does not pressure people to conform; allows for doubt, seeking, and vulnerability. Accepts people as they are. Feels safe to be yourself. "Take what you like and leave the rest."
Individual needs are ignored, unless they are of the leader. Focus is outside of the group, in converting others or in the future. Denial of personal needs is expected to carry on work of group.	Balances a focus on growth for the most people, with respecting individual needs. Focus on the present; bodily needs, emotions, and inner voice respected as a source of wisdom.
Gossip is common under the guise of "care for others."	Anonymity and privacy are respected; the members and what they share is not discussed.
Those outside the group are "othered"; common enemy belonging may be a binding force. Stereotypes are in common use to justify "othering."	Group is inclusive and does not reject anyone regardless of type of status. People are regarded as individuals, not as representatives of any group.

Bad Communities for Personal Growth	*Good Communities for Personal Growth*
Elevates some people over others; some people have higher privileges than others. Double standard for leaders and participants; leaders don't embody the characteristics they require of followers. Requires unquestioning and inappropriate loyalty to leader.	Recognizes individual gifts but doesn't worship them. Leaders walk the talk and are working on the same issues as the participants; same standards apply to all. Leaders and participants are all expected to embody the characteristics described in chapter 15 (also listed below). May have rotation of leadership.
Care for others is conditional upon belonging, belief, or behavior. Exploits members in some way—perhaps sexually or financially.	Care for others in group is real, no matter what they have done.
Leaders or members are self-satisfied.	Leader and members are seeking constant improvement, not content to stay still.
	Is joyful.

But importantly, although you shouldn't feel pressure to join or to conform, being with a group that is healthy should change you. In a healthy group, you should grow closer and closer to the person that you are meant to be.

The characteristics to look for in chapter 15 are humility, peacefulness, defined boundaries, awareness of their own bias and working to detach from it, valuing equality, assumes good intentions, and wants to learn from others.

This chapter is just an introduction to what to look for in this type of community. You may find what you need in an organization you already belong to, or you may need to search for one. A list of organizations who have some of the characteristics that provide support for people who are working on their own issues or that are already working in similar areas can be found in the appendix. Use this chapter to determine whether the organizations you are already part of will be able to provide support for you. If not, you may need to start your own group. Help for doing that can be found in the separate volume, *Persuade, Don't Preach: A Leader's Guide.* Or you can join one of the online communities being created. Join the waiting list for a community by emailing Karen at info@ethical-frames.com.

21
THE ETHICS OF
PERSUADING

A S I HAVE been working on these concepts, I kept pondering whether what I was proposing was ethical. After all, one of the reasons I went to seminary was to explore ethical behavior. I kept thinking that this technique could be used to manipulate people. And while it could be used to manipulate people, I can't control that. But it will be hard to manipulate people without really understanding them, so perhaps that is a satisfactory goal, to reach the Ethical Zone of understanding.

The real test will be if people feel manipulated and unhappy with the result, then it is unethical. I think you can see about the issue of same-sex marriage that they don't feel that they were badly used. If we can see people as separate from how they feel about the issues and their Ethical Zone Framework, then we will treat people differently.

Robb Willer brought up the issue of respect in his TED Talk. His prescription of what is needed to solve the problems is to have "empathy and respect, empathy and respect." That raises the question of whether this technique is respectful, and the answer to that is yes. When we preach, we are being disrespectful.

I have run into people who are such strong believers in their issue that they aren't open to new ideas and aren't open to hearing what other people think. Fanatics won't be able to achieve the Ethical Zone of understanding because they are so caught up in their own reality, they can't see anyone else's truth as important. That's not ethical in my book. That's the second part of my answer as to whether this is manipulative; it is manipulative if you are not open to being changed yourself.

Another issue is whether using fear as a motivating force is ethical. You may have noticed that I rarely used fear in my reframing examples. My conclusion is that using fear of people is definitely unethical, and it is also not ethical to use the fear of change that Conservatives have against them. However, using fear of events (provided they are not related to who people are or what they do) can be appropriate.

For example, fear of disease is appropriate for antivaxxers and fear of a hurricane or tsunami or earthquake is appropriate for evacuation efforts. Which brings me to the issue of climate change, which is a future event and contentious. In that case, fear will only work for those who already believe it, so fear of climate change won't work except among those who are already in your choir. If you want to convince the unbelievers, fear won't work. It will backfire.

We need to separate the people from the issues from their Ethical Zones. We can disagree about issues and respect people and their Ethical Zones.

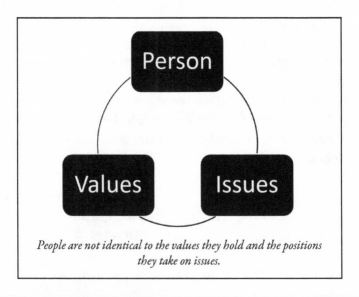

People are not identical to the values they hold and the positions they take on issues.

We need to separate the people from the issues from their Ethical Zones. We can disagree about issues and respect people and their Ethical Zones.

But one more question is relevant. This question was adopted by Citigroup after the financial crisis to ensure that the decisions like the ones that led to the crisis were never made again. The question is this: Is it systemically responsible? Is what I am proposing going to lead to increased divisions in society or more bridges across those divides? I believe it will increase the bridges.

I want this book to be used for virtuous ends. I want these concepts to lead to peace flourishing. Help me make that a reality. Use the information in this book responsibly.

APPENDIX

THESE ORGANIZATIONS ARE supportive to people who want to do things differently (such as the changes I call for in this book), even if they don't explicitly say so

12 step Groups

The most well-known 12 step group is the first, Alcoholics Anonymous. Less well known are its many spin-offs. The benefits of 12 step groups is that you meet people who are very different than you are in a structured setting in which you all have one characteristic in common—whatever the focus is of that group.

There are groups for those who have been affected by someone else's drinking, for people who grew up in a dysfunctional family, for people who have trouble with emotions, for people who have gambling or other money problems. I highly recommend 12 step recovery groups to anyone, whether you have an active drinker in your life or not. These groups are a tremendous complement to therapy. If this is interesting to you, find one you qualify for and experience it yourself. You will find people who accept you as you are and who will support you along this journey.

Privilege Conference

A black-owned conference that runs once a year, changing locations every year. Creates a sense of community among people of all races, with a shared sense of letting each other try new behaviors and being okay with making mistakes. I attended once and learned a lot about myself and the blinders I had on. Can act as a counterpoint to the duality mindset and to the fear of being called out if you make a mistake.

Heterodox Academy

Created out of Jonathan Haidt's calling out of the colleges not being tolerant of Conservative culture. Meets once a year. Primarily composed of academics and a few students. Once a year conference held in New York City. It's a terrific way to hear examples of people trying out new ways.

Open Mind Platform

Based on Dr. Haidt's research and other psychological research, this platform has been created to help a group become less politically polarized. I have not used it. It is available for nonprofits at no charge: https://openmindplatform.org/.

Better Angels

From their website: Better Angels is a national citizens' movement to reduce political polarization in the United States by bringing Liberals and Conservatives together to understand each other beyond stereotypes, forming red/blue community alliances, teaching practical skills for communicating across political differences, and making a strong public argument for depolarization.

I have no experience with this organization. I have heard from someone who has participated that they have trouble recruiting Conservatives: https://www.better-angels.org/our-story/#our-approach.

Center for Nonviolent Communication

Although not specifically focused on politics, the skills taught by this group can be useful preparation. I have attended a weekend training: https://www.cnvc.org/trainings.

Ethical Frames Workshops

Building on the principles outlined in the book, Ethical Frames LLC has created workshops that help create a supportive community for change. To join the waiting list to participate in an online workshop, send an email to Info@ethicalframes.com.

AFTERWARD

I WRITE THIS particular afterward in October 2020, right after President Trump has been diagnosed with COVID-19. Although President Trump is behind in the polls, the election outcome is up the air. But even after the election, the problems posed by political polarization aren't going to go away; they'll still exist.

And the problems aren't just political. They've bled into our personal relationships. Long-standing relationships of all types are being broken, fractured by the rancor that accompanies our political divide. Politics is tearing apart families, neighborhoods, workplaces. As I've been working on this book and my newsletter, *Mending Fractured Relationships*, I've encountered stories of adult children breaking with their parents over politics, co-workers who formerly got along no longer speaking, neighbors who have stopped speaking to one another, and more.

Politics has been tearing at the relationships that are the very fabric of our society, and we'll be dealing with the reverberations of this for a long time to come.

How can we heal? I would like to suggest that we need to mend those fractured personal relationships, one at a time. We each need to invest time in rebuilding those relationships. To do that, we need new tools. The old ones aren't sufficient; they got us into this mess.

I hope after reading this book you have a better understanding of what is driving these divisions and have an inkling of tools that can help. But it isn't easy work. As I continue to talk to people about the relationships that have been affected, I try to make suggestions based on the theories in this book. But, people often just shrug because they're so discouraged and tired. Or they get angry. They don't have hope.

I need to believe that there is still hope. It helps when I remember the example of how Northern Ireland came together. If you remember, during the Troubles, the Protestants and Catholics had been killing each other since the 1960s, setting bombs, until they managed to sit down together. The Good Friday Agreement was passed in 1998 after years of talks. It was passed by a majority vote of the citizens and it has held for over two decades. If they can do that, we can too here in the United States.

But we can only put our country together if we can put our relationships together.

Talking about politics itself isn't the answer. We need to talk about the issues *behind* the politics; we need to learn to appreciate what the other side brings that we don't have.

I'm not a politician. I have no power base. But I have some ideas of steps we can take to get closer to healing.

What can help is learning from examples and building a community to support people who want to do this type of work.

My newsletter, *Mending Fractured Relationships*, is an ongoing collection of stories about those relationships in our lives that have become broken because of politics. Based on those stories and the theories I'm working with, I provide suggestions for what might work to help repair those relationships.

In order for these methods to work, we need ongoing support. When you try new things, you often fail the first time and might be tempted to give up. But if you have a community to practice with and to check in with, you're more likely to reach success.

If you have a supportive community that's great. But if you don't, join mine. Email me at info@ethicalframes.com to join the waiting list for my community.

Somebody has to start. I hope you're up for the challenge. Join me in this effort.

Want to learn more about how to *Persuade, Don't Preach*?

The workbook with exercises to practice taking another perspective and reframing is in press and will be available soon.

Also, coming soon: The leader's guide for those who want to create groups to support the work needed for *Persuade, Don't Preach*.

Also check the website www.Persuadedontpreach.com for Karen Tibbals's talks and workshops near you. Or you can arrange for Karen to talk to your group by emailing her at info@ethicalframes.com.

REFERENCES

Amin, A. et al. 2017. "Association of Moral Values with Vaccine Hesitancy." *Nature Human Behaviour* 1 (12): 873–880.

Anderson, N. et al. 2017. "Differentiating Emotional Processing and Attention in Psychopathy with Functional Neuroimaging." *Cogn Affect Behav Neurosci* 17: 491–515.

Babiak, Paul. 2006. *Snakes in Suits.* New York: Regan.

Brown, Brené. 2017. *Braving the Wilderness.* New York: Random House.

Byung-Chul, Han. 2015. *The Transparency Society.* 1st Edition. Stanford Briefs.

Case, Ann and Angus Deaton. 2017. Mortality and Morbidity in the 21ST Century. Brookings. Accessed 2 22, 2020. https://www.brookings.edu/bpea-articles/mortality-and-morbidity-in-the-21st-century/.

Caspar, Emile, Axel Cleremans, and Patrick Haggard. 2018. "Only Giving Orders? An Experimental Study of the Sense of Agency When Giving or Receiving Commands." *PLoS One* 13(9).

Curtis, Valerie. 2013. *Don't Look, Don't Touch, Don't Eat. The Science behind Revulsion.* Chicago: University of Chicago.

Deaton, Angus. 2013. *The Great Escape: Health, Wealth, and the Origins of Inequality.* Princeton: Princeton University.

DeVinney, Timothy M., Pat Auger, and Giana M. Eckhardt. 2010. *The Myth of the Ethical Consumer.* Cambridge: Cambridge University Press.

Dobin, Arthur. 2012. "It's Not Fair! But What Is Fairness?" May 11.

Accessed 11 3, 2018. https://www.psychologytoday.com/us/blog/am-i-right/201205/its-not-fair-what-is-fairness.

Economist. 2019. "Brothers in Alms." *The Economist*. p. 40. Dec. 14.

Economist. 2019. "The Self-Preservation Society." *The Economist*. pp. 16–19. July 6.

Economist. 2020. "Business Has Gone Sour in America's Dairy Capital." *The Economist*. p. 25. January 25

Edgecliffe-Johnson, Andrew. 2018. "Nike Picks a Side in America's Culture Wars." Sept. 7. Accessed 9 8, 2018. https://www.ft.com/content/c774408a-b275-11e8-8d14-6f049d06439c.

Edsall, Thomas B. 2012. "Let the Nanotargeting Begin." *New York Times*, April 15.

Feinberg, M. et al. In press. "Extreme Protest Tactics Reduce Popular Support for Social Movements." *Journal of Personality and Social Psychology*. Accessed 1 31, 2020.. https://27e75f17-be37-4c64-91ba-77473583e74a.filesusr.com/ugd/2f07d4_d1b383ca663043478d5879eee8708db3.pdf.

FiveThirtyEight.com. 2020. "How Unpopular Is Donald Trump?" *FiveThirtyEight.com*. Accessed 2 12. 2020. https://projects.fivethirtyeight.com/trump-approval-ratings/.

Friedman, Nancy. 2013. "The Ads We Deserve." June 25. Accessed 9 8, 2018. https://www.vocabulary.com/articles/candlepwr/the-ads-we-deserve/.

Gopnik, Alison. 2013. "How Early Do We Learn Racial Us Versus Them?" *Wall Street Journal*, May 18: C2.

Gopnik, Alison. 2013. "Implicit Racial Bias in Children." *Alisongopnik.com*. http://alisongopnik.com/Alison_Gopnik_WSJcolumns.htm#21Apr13.

Gopnick, Alison. 2014. "Even Children Get More Outraged at Us Versus Them." *Wall Street Journal*, August 17.

Grabar, H. 2018. "The Road to Nowhere." Slate.com June 19. Accessed 1

31, 2020 https://slate.com/business/2018/06/americans-are-moving-less-often-than-ever.html.

Graves, Clare. 1981. *Summary Statement: The Emergent Cyclical Double-Helix Model of the Adult Human Biopsychosocial Systems.* Accessed 2 12, 2020. http://www.clarewgraves.com/articles_content/1981_handout/1981_summary.pdf.

Gerson, M. 2019. "Politics Is Religion, and the Right Is Getting Ready for the End Times." *Washington Post.* March 18.

Greene, Joshua. 2013. *Moral Tribes: Emotion, Reason and the Gap between Us and Them.* New York: Penguin.

Greene, Joshua. 2014. "The Cognitive Neuroscience of Moral Judgment and Decision-Making." In *The Cognitive Neurosciences V*, edited by Gazzaniga. M. Cambridge: MIT Press.

Greenleaf, Robert. 1977. *Servant Leadership.* New York: Paulist Press.

Haidt, Jonathan. 2012. *The Righteous Mind.* New York: Vintage.

Hare, Robert. 1993. *Without Conscience: The Disturbing World of Psychopaths among Us.* New York: Penguin.

Hari, Johann. 2018. *Lost Connections.* New York: Bloomsbury.

Hetherington, Marc, and Jonathan Weiler. 2018. *Prius or Pickup?* Boston: Houghton Mifflin Harcourt.

Hibbing, John R., Hevin B. Smith, and John A. Alford. 2014. *Predisposed.* New York and London: Routledge.

Hillyer, Q. 2019. "Why I Remain a Never Trumper, and What It Means." *Washington Examiner.* March 11. Accessed 1 31, 2020 https://www.washingtonexaminer.com/opinion/columnists/why-i-remain-a-never-trumper-and-what-it-means.

Holland, Sarah Stewart and Beth Silvers. 2019. *I Think You're Wrong (But I'm Listening): A Guide to Grace-Filled Political Conversations.* Nashville: Thomas Nelson.

Jones, Van. 2017. *Beyond the Messy Truth. How We Came Apart. How We Come Together.* New York: Ballantine.

Kahneman, Daniel. 2011. *Thinking, Fast and Slow*. New York: Farrar, Strauss, Giroux.

Kangeisser, Patricia, and Felix Warneken. 2012. "Young Children Consider Merit when Sharing Resources." *PLoS One* 7(8).

Kappes, A. et al. 2019. "Confirmation Bias in the Utilization of Others' Opinion Strength." *Nature Neuroscience.* Accessed 1 31, 2020 https://www.nature.com/articles/s41593-019-0549-2.

Keane, M. et al. 2005. "Confidence in Vaccination." *Vaccine* 23 (19): 2486–93.

Knowles, Eric, and Sarah DiMuccio. 2018. "How Donald Trump Appeals to Men Secretly Insecure about Their Manhood." *Washington Post.* Nov. 29. Accessed 12 9, 2018. https://www.washingtonpost.com/news/monkey-cage/wp/2018/11/29/how-donald-trump-appeals-to-men-secretly-insecure-about-their-manhood/?utm_term=.f071de8494b7.

Konnikova, Maria. 2016. "How We Learn Fairness." *New Yorker.* January 7. https://www.newyorker.com/science/maria-konnikova/how-we-learn-fairness.

Markovitch, Noam, Liam Netzer, and Maya Tamir. 2016. "Will You Touch a Dirty Diaper? Attitudes toward Disgust and Behavior." *Cognition and Emotion* 30 (3): 592–602.

Mason, Lilliana. 2018. *Uncivil Agreement: How Politics Became Our Identity.* Chicago: University of Chicago.

McAfee, Andrew. 2019. *More from Less: The Surprising Story of How We Learned to Prosper Using Fewer Resources—and What Happens Next.* New York & London: Simon & Schuster.

McAuliffe, Katherine, Peter Blake, and Felix Warneken. 2017. "Do Kids Have a Fundamental Sense of Fairness?" *Scientific American.* August 23. Accessed 1 31, 2020 https://blogs.scientificamerican.com/observations/do-kids-have-a-fundamental-sense-of-fairness/.

McDonald, J., D. Karol, and L. Mason. 2019. "Many Voters Think Trump Is a Self-made Man.

What Happens When You Tell Them Otherwise?" *Politico.* Accessed 1
31, 2020 https://www.politico.com/magazine/story/2019/01/17/
many-voters-think-trumps-a-self-made-man-what-happens-when-
you-tell-them-otherwise-224019.

Mooney, Chris. 2012. *Republican Brain.* Hoboken: Wiley.

Morales, Angela et al. 2012. "How Disgust Enhances the Effectiveness of
Fear Appeals." *Journal of Marketing Research V* XLIX: 383–393.

Mycoskie, Blake. 2016. "How I Did It: The Founder of Tom's on
Reimagining the Company's Vision." *Harvard Business Review,* Janu-
ary-February: 41–44.

Myers, Vernā. (n.d.) "How to Overcome Our Biases." Accessed 1 31,
2020 https://www.ted.com/talks/verna_myers_how_to_overcome_
our_biases_walk_boldly_toward_them?language=en.

Perry, Gina. 2013. *Behind the Shock Machine: The Untold Story of the
Notorious Milgram Psychology Experiments.* New York: New Press.

Pew Research Center. 2017. "How the Political Typology Groups Compare." Accessed 1 31, 2020. https://www.people-press.org/
interactives/political-typology-comparison-2017/?issue=americas-
openness.

Pinker, Steven. 2011. *Better Angels of Our Nature: Why Violence Has
Declined.* New York: Viking.

Pinker, Steven. 2018. *Enlightenment Now.* New York: Viking.

Putnam, Robert. 2000. *Bowling Alone.* New York: Simon & Schuster.

Raglan, G. et al. 2014. "Need to Know: The Need for Cognitive Closure
Impacts the Clinical Practice of Obstetrician/Gynecologists." *BMC
Medical Informatics and Decision Making* 14:122.

Ritter, Ryan et al. 2016. "Imagine No Religion: Heretical Disgust, Anger
and the Symbolic Purity of Mind." *Cognition and Emotion* 30 (4):
778–796.

Rozin, Paul, Jonathan Haidt, and Clark McCauley. 2008. "Disgust." In
Handbook of Emotions, 3rd edition, edited by Jeannette M. Haviland-

Jones, Lisa Feldman Barrett, and Michael Lewis, 757–76. New York: The Guildford Press.

Sapolsky, Robert M. 2017. *Behave: The Biology of Humans at Our Best and Worst*. New York: Penguin Press.

Sashkin, Marshall, and Molly G. Sashkin. 2013. *Leadership that Matters: The Critical Factors for Making a Difference in People's Lives and Organizational Success*. San Francisco: Berrett-Koehler.

Scheepers, Daan, and Belle Derks. 2016. "Revisiting Social Identity Theory from a Neuroscience Perspective." *Current Opinion in Psychology* 11: 74–78.

Scholz & Friends. 2009. "The Other Side of America." August 12. Accessed 11 5, 2018. https://www.adsoftheworld.com/media/print/queer_the_other_side_of_america.

Schrope, M. 2013. "Nuclear Power Prevents More Deaths Than It Causes." *Chemical and Engineering News*. Accessed 1 31, 2019 https://cen.acs.org/articles/91/web/2013/04/Nuclear-Power-Prevents-Deaths-Causes.html.

Schweizer, Peter. 2008. *Makers and Takers: Why Conservatives work harder, feel happier, have closer families, take fewer drugs, give more generously, value honesty more, are less materialistic and envious, whine less...and even hug their children more than liberals*. New York: Doubleday.

Shrimp, Terrence, and Elenora Stuart. 2004. "The Role of Disgust as an Emotional Mediator of Advertising Effects." *Journal of Advertising* 33 (1): 43–53.

Skitka, Linda, and Anthony Washburn. 2013. *Are Conservatives from Mars and Liberals from Venus?* Claremont.

Smith, N. 2020. **"**"Why Hostility to Immigration Runs So Deep." January 13. Bloomberg. Accessed 1 31, 2020 https://www.bloomberg.com/opinion/articles/2020-01-13/why-hostility-to-immigration-runs-so-deep-in-developed-nations.

Tenzer, A. 2019. "The Collapse of Context." *The Drum*. Accessed 1 31,

2020 https://www.thedrum.com/opinion/2019/04/29/the-collapse-context-seeing-through-the-promise-social-media-community-building.

Thaler, Richard, and Cass Sunstein. 2008. *Nudge.* New Haven: Yale University Press.

Tracy, Jessica L., Conor M. Steckler, and Gordon Heltzel. (n.d.) "The Physiological Basis of Psychological Disgust and Moral Judgments." *University of British Columbia.* Accessed 12 10, 2018. http://ubc-emotionlab.ca/wp-content/files_mf/tracystecklerheltzelinpressjpsp.pdf.

Velasquez-Manoff, M. 2019. Want to be less racist? Move to Hawaii. *New York Times Sunday Review.* Accessed 2 12, 2020. https://www.nytimes.com/2019/06/28/opinion/sunday/racism-hawaii.html.

Voekel, J. and M. Weinberg. 2018. "Morally Reframed Arguments Can Affect Support for Political Candidates." *Social Psychological and Personality Science.* Vol. 9 (8) 917–24.

Waldemar, Christian. 2018. "Does Social Media Cause Depression?" *Psych Central.* Accessed 1 31, 2020 https://psychcentral.com/blog/does-social-media-cause-depression/.

Wilbur, Ken. 2001. *A Brief History of Everything.* Boston: Shambala.

Willer, Robb, and Matthew Feinberg. 2015. "From Gulf to Bridge: When Do Moral Arguments Facilitate Political Influence?" *Personality and Social Psychology Bulletin* 1-17.

Willer, R. and J. Voekel. 2019. **"Why Progressive Candidates Should Invoke Conservative Values." *New York Times Sunday Review*. Accessed 1 31, 2020 https://www.nytimes.com/2019/11/30/opinion/sunday/progressive-candidates-conservative-values.html.**

Yourmorals.org. 2016. *Moral Foundations.* Accessed 11 3, 2018. https://moralfoundations.org/.

ACKNOWLEDGMENTS

I WANT TO thank my friends, family members, and former colleagues for their encouragement and feedback. Denis's and Chris's willingness to act as sounding boards is greatly appreciated. The help with graphics from Laura Hoesly was immensely useful.

I especially want to thank my Monday morning and Saturday morning support groups and my Quaker Meeting in Plainfield, New Jersey, where I experienced the positive sides of belonging, community, and leadership. All of them have been instrumental in helping me grow as a person and becoming closer to the person that God wants me to be.

I also want to specifically thank the faculty of the Earlham School of Religion, especially Steve Angell and Lonnie Valentine, who, among many others, encouraged me to develop my voice.

I also deeply appreciate the people who gave of their time and expertise by reading drafts of my first book and providing me valuable feedback: Mark Ross, Anne Camille Talley, Chuck Merkel, Arlene Johnson, Bill Harvey, and Dick Vanderveer. Also, thanks to those who helped me shape an even earlier work: Dan Reilly, Claudia Kienzle, Andy Kienzle, Krystal Odell, John Odell, Chris Cleary, and Laura Hoesly.

I also want to acknowledge those who attended my presentations on this latest book at Earlham School of Religion, Plainfield-Shrewsbury Half Yearly Meeting, Orlando Friends Meeting, Plainfield Friends Meeting, and the libraries in Piscataway and Franklin Township NJ. From your questions and concerns, I learned what was working and what could be improved.

And to the enthusiastic support of my advanced readers, I owe a debt of gratitude. Thanks to Steven Ross for believing in me. Susan Jeffers put a lot of effort into her critique and helped me sharpen some sections. Patricia Kane gave me new language to describe what this book does for people.

My editor, Sandra Wendel; copywriter, Kim Ledgerwood; and designer, Elizabeth Gethering all provided skills that I don't have and value, thank you.

There are also a set of people who have influenced me over time, many of them through their public personas, who are too numerous to mention here but are mentioned throughout the text. Thank you for your thoughtful work.

ABOUT
THE AUTHOR

K AREN J. TIBBALS is a dedicated researcher and writer who focuses on information that can help people improve their lives.

She holds an MBA in marketing from Rutgers University and an MA in religion from Earlham School of Religion.

Before leaving her corporate career to go back to school, she used her research skills to help the major multinational companies she worked for market products to consumers and doctors. She helped launch pharmaceutical products for high blood pressure, schizophrenia, and asthma in the US.

Her first book, *Marketing Landmines: The Next Generation of Emotional Branding* (2019), is about how to apply principles of recent social science to marketing. Before that, her research has focused on how people apply their beliefs to their business life with a thesis entitled *The Theological Basis behind Quaker Businesses.*

Her previous publications include the chapter on "Early Quakers and Just Debt" in the volume *Quakers Business and Industry* and the chapter titled "The Quaker Employer Conference of 1918" in *Quakers, Business and Corporate Responsibility,* and contributions to two journal publications: Confidence in Vaccination and Patient Counseling Materials.

She has given her engaging, interactive presentations at universities, churches, libraries, conferences, and corporations. Her talks focus on how to apply the principles of Ethical Zones Framework to marketing, management, ethics, politics, and everyday life. She has also created a newsletter to showcase stories of how our political polarization is affecting our everyday lives, and to provide examples of how the tools described in this book can be used.

To contact her about speaking or workshops, email Karen at Info@ethicalframes.com.

CPSIA information can be obtained
at www.ICGtesting.com
Printed in the USA
LVHW031250051221
705331LV00006B/1107